Love Laughs

A Playful Guide to Deepening Your Romantic Connection

Funny conversation starters, activities for couples, and romantic
ideas for date nights and beyond

By, Avery Carter

This book is dedicated to **Mabel,** *who*
inspires romance every day

Table of Contents

Introduction

Writing "Love Laughs: A Playful Guide to Deepening Your Romantic Connection" has been a journey filled with joy, reflection, and discovery. As someone who has always cherished the beauty of human connection, crafting this book was not just about sharing ideas—it was about celebrating the laughter, the quirks, and the magical moments that make love such a profound experience. In a new relationship and having experienced the end of other relationships, I was inspired to become more intentional about getting to know my partner and enjoying shared experiences. I believe that romance isn't just about grand gestures or sweeping declarations; it's about the small, intentional moments that allow us to see, understand, and appreciate one another more deeply.

This book was born from the desire to help couples kindle or rekindle their spark and nurture their connection in a world that often feels too busy, distracted, or serious. Whether you're in the early stages of love or years into your relationship, keeping the laughter alive and the connection thriving takes effort, creativity, and a willingness to try new things. And that's exactly what this book aims to offer. Find a new hobby together or discover that you both hate the same new experience. Wherever these activities lead you, enjoy the ride together.

At its heart, "Love Laughs" is a playful guide designed to breathe fresh air into your relationship. The first cornerstone of the book is a collection of 54 unique and fun activity ideas presented in a "recipe" format. These activities aren't just about having a good time—they're about fostering a deeper understanding of each other, building trust, and creating shared memories that will bring you closer. From whimsical date night ideas to creative ways to learn more about your partner's inner world, these suggestions are here to inspire you to think outside the box and reconnect in meaningful ways.

The second pillar of this book is the conversation starter prompts that accompany each activity. I've always believed that communication is the heartbeat of any thriving relationship. But let's face it: even the most in-love couples can find themselves stuck in the rut of everyday small talk. These prompts are designed to take you out of the mundane and into the magical, sparking discussions that lead to laughter, vulnerability, and perhaps even surprising discoveries about one another. With questions that range from lighthearted to deeply introspective, this section is an invitation to rediscover your partner, one conversation at a time.

Finally, the book is sprinkled with romance stories—both from everyday couples and historically significant love affairs. These anecdotes remind us that love takes on many forms and expressions, but at its core, it is always transformative. From the ordinary joys of a couple's weekend-getaway to the timeless passion of historical icons, these stories are here to inspire, entertain, and remind us of the endless possibilities that love holds.

What I hope you take from this book is not just a list of ideas or prompts, but a renewed sense of playfulness and possibility in your relationship. I want you to laugh together, to try new things, to embrace the silly and the serious in equal measure. More than anything, I hope this book helps you carve out space in your lives to truly see and cherish one another, even amidst life's chaos.

Love is a journey, and like any great adventure, it's best navigated with curiosity, creativity, and a sense of humor. My wish for you, as you explore the pages of "Love Laughs," is that you find new ways to deepen your connection, celebrate your unique bond, and, of course, share countless moments of laughter along the way.

Thank you for allowing me to be a part of your love story.

Avery

Operation Love Note

What you'll need

- **Notepaper or 100 Post-its:** You can spread love messages throughout the house or fill an entire room with notes.
- **Red Marker, Colored Pencils, or Favorite Pen:** The writing tool that makes you feel you're most expressive. Add some extra color to bring your words to life.
- **Your Romantic Imagination:** The more heartfelt, the better. You're writing from the soul, after all.
- **Craft Supplies:** Stickers, stamps, or even glitter. Get as crafty as you like.

Directions

Get Inspired: Before writing, think about your partner and what makes your relationship unique. Is it the way they laugh at your jokes? How do they always know when you need a hug? Think about those moments that make your heart swell and use them to guide your message.

Create Your Love Note: Write a heartfelt message to your partner, whether a short and sweet "I love you" or a more extended ode to your shared journey. If you're feeling extra artistic, sketch a picture or create a pictogram to add an extra layer of fun. You could even write a series of notes leading your partner to a surprise or tell a story when read sequentially.

Hide the Note: Now comes the sneaky part. Place your note somewhere unexpected where your partner will find it. Try their lunchbox, tucked inside their favorite book, in the fridge on their snack of choice, or taped to the bathroom mirror. Be creative with the placement to increase the element of surprise.

Add a Twist: Take your love note game up a notch by using it to set up a romantic rendezvous. Drop a hint in the note about meeting in a particular spot—a candlelit dinner, a cozy blanket under the stars, or a hot chocolate date on the living room couch. Let the note be a clue that leads to an evening they won't forget.

Spice It Up

Create a Love Note Treasure Hunt: Write a series of notes that lead your partner from one location to the next, giving each note a clue to the next hiding spot. End the hunt with a heartfelt message and a small gift, such as a favorite snack, a movie you've been meaning to watch together, or a massage voucher (redeemable immediately, of course).

Make It a Regular Thing: Turn love notes into a weekly or monthly tradition. Surprise each other with notes in random places or keep a dedicated "love note jar" where you drop your messages for your partner to find. Over time, you'll build a collection that captures your journey together.

Why It Matters

Flirting with your partner and leaving love notes isn't just cute; it's proven to strengthen relationships. It fosters connection, boosts happiness, and deepens emotional intimacy. The simple act of writing down your feelings can be a powerful reminder of what you cherish most about each other.

Conversation Starters

- What's the most memorable surprise you've planned or received?

- When was the last time you did something romantic just because?
- What would it say if you could write one note that your partner would read repeatedly?

Operation Love Note is your mission to keep the romance alive, one thoughtful message at a time. Whether you're a poet, a doodler, or a person of few words, there's no wrong way to express your love. Just dive in, get creative, and enjoy the journey.

Game Night with a Twist

What you'll need

A Game:

- Deck of Cards
- Twister for Two (clothes optional)
- Sex Dice
- Would You Rather (adult version)

Game Night Outfit:

- Skintight Sexy
- Serious Athlete
- Game Night Nerd

Set-Up:

- Candlelight / Firelight
- A Cocktail - Hydrate
- Snacks - Power Up
- Pump Up Playlist
- Chalk Scoreboard

Directions

Unlock a world of playful rivalry and intimate exploration with the ultimate game night for two! Deep dive into the spirit of competition, but with a saucy, affectionate twist that promises more than just a few laughs to set the mood, send your partner a tantalizing invitation—whether it's a flirty note left on their pillow or a sultry text message that hints at an evening filled with giggles and whispers. The fun starts before the first game is even played!

Whether you're a seasoned board game aficionado or card game novice, the real magic lies in discovering new facets of your relationship. Celebrate victories with kisses, and let losses become playful dares or challenges. And if you're looking to spice things up, introduce a cheeky rule that turns an ordinary game into an enticing flirtation that could go anywhere.

For example, how about: "Whenever someone wins a round, they get to ask the other a daring 'Would You Rather?' question with a saucy twist."

As the evening unfolds, remember the importance of ambiance. Dim the lights, get cozy by a fire, and play your favorite playlist to keep the energy upbeat. Whether it's playful background tunes or your favorite love songs, the music will set the rhythm for the night. Keep a cocktail within reach—preferably one that brings out your adventurous side—and munch on snacks that energize, like chocolate-covered strawberries or spiced nuts. A little fuel keeps the competition lively!

Spice it Up

Why stop at simple rules? Make the night even more memorable by setting a few "house rules" that up the ante. For instance, add a rule where every time one of you rolls a double, they must share a fantasy or an intimate compliment. Or, if a card lands on an odd number, the person must choose between answering a secret question or revealing something unexpected about themselves. Remember, the goal is to keep things light, fun, and flirtatious—nothing too serious!

Don't Forget the Goal

While the scoreboard might keep track of points, tonight's true objective is sparking joy, sharing laughter, and cozying up with your favorite teammate. The best part! In this game, there's no such thing as losing; it's all about winning in love. So, play each game with a wink and a smile because you're both on the winning team tonight, no matter what the score says.

Conversation Starters

- What was the best night you ever spent together?
- What made that night so special?
- If you could relive one romantic moment, which would it be and why?

End the night with a toast to love, laughter, and new memories. After all, as Eva Gabor said, "Love is a game that two can play, and both win by losing their heart."

Love Quest Scavenger Hunt

What You'll Need

Clues:

- Simple notecards with riddles or memories
- A mini puzzle with a personalized picture as the solution
- A crossword template with words that are special to your relationship.
- A hand-drawn map leading to different clue locations or even a treasure map-style sketch.

The Treasure:

- A thoughtful gift, like a handwritten love letter or a small piece of jewelry
- A poem written just for your partner.
- An itinerary for a surprise activity, like a movie night or day trip
- Tickets to an upcoming concert or play or a gift certificate for a shared experience (like a cooking class or dance lesson)

Directions

Begin the adventure with a mysterious note or puzzle that sets the tone for your scavenger hunt. Each clue should lead to the next with creativity and intrigue, weaving a story that only you can unravel. Here are some ideas for clues and how to incorporate them:

Riddles or Rhymes: Write a poem or riddle that hints at the next clue's location. For example: *"Where love wishes are whispered and* *coins take flight, seek the well where dreams feel right. Toss a thought and linger a spell; your next clue is found at the well."*

Hidden Messages in Ordinary Places: Slip a clue inside a hollowed-out fruit or vegetable in the fridge, or even tape it inside a book on your partner's nightstand.

Crosswords or Word Jumbles: Create a crossword puzzle in which the answers relate to shared experiences or inside jokes. When solved, the puzzle will reveal a secret phrase leading to the following location.

A Picture Says a Thousand Words: Use a mini puzzle created from a photo of a memorable place and scatter the pieces throughout the house for your partner to find. Once completed, the image will hint at the next clue's location.

Mystery in a Map: Draw a map using symbols or illustrations that are meaningful to your relationship. For instance, the map could mark the spot where you first met, first said, "I love you," or even your favorite place for a coffee date.

Spice It Up

- To make the hunt even more special, you can add unique and personal touches to the clues and the final treasure:
- **Memory Lane Theme:** Each clue could reference a special moment in your relationship. For instance, one clue could be hidden where you first met and the next where you first said, "I love you." At each location, leave a small memento or photo from that time.
- **Surprise Detours:** Occasionally, let a clue lead to a detour, like making your partner complete a fun or silly task (e.g., doing a dance move or singing a favorite song together) before giving the next hint. This adds an element of playfulness and excitement to the experience.

- **Romantic Gestures Throughout** Scatter small, romantic surprises at some clue locations—like a rose petal trail, chocolate treats, or love notes to give your partner an extra dose of sweetness along the journey.

Conversation Starters

- To make the scavenger hunt more than just a game, consider incorporating prompts or questions along the way to spark meaningful conversations. Here are some additional starters:
- *What is your favorite memory of us, and why does it stand out?*
- *If you could relive any moment in our relationship, which would it be and why?*
- *Describe a perfect day for you that includes me. What would we do?*
- *What qualities in a relationship do you find most important, and how do we embody those together?*

Soothe & Spoil Massage

A massage night is more than just a pampering experience—it's an opportunity to connect, relax, and share meaningful moments with your partner. Turn your living space into a sanctuary of tranquility and romance where you can escape from the everyday hustle and focus on each other. Follow these steps for an unforgettable night of relaxation, intimacy, and connection.

What You'll Need

- Luxurious massage oil or lotion (look for one with a scent you both enjoy, like lavender, sandalwood, or vanilla)
- Scented candles (choose calming scents like chamomile, eucalyptus, or jasmine)
- A relaxing or romantic playlist (soft instrumental music, nature sounds, or slow acoustic tunes)
- A timer (to help keep the massage balanced and flowing)
- Your choice of a soothing drink:
  - A Hot Toddy to warm up on a chilly night
  - A Lavender Lemonade Cocktail to refresh on a warm evening

Directions

Set the Scene: Transform your room into a peaceful retreat. Dim the lights, light the scented candles, and play your carefully curated playlist. Ensure the room is warm enough for comfort but not overly hot, as you want to create a cozy and inviting atmosphere. A warm towel draped over your partner's body can also help them feel snug.

Cocktail Time: Depending on the season or your mood, choose a hot toddy or lavender lemonade cocktail. These drinks will help you unwind and set a relaxing tone for the evening. Sip slowly and enjoy the flavor while appreciating each other's company.

Massage Time: Decide who will go first and take turns massaging each other. The focus should be on how your partner is feeling. Use a timer if needed, setting it to 10-15-minute intervals for different areas of the body. Start with the shoulders and neck and gradually work down to the back, arms, legs, and feet. Pay attention to the pressure you're using, adjusting it based on your partner's preferences. Keep the strokes slow and steady to encourage more profound relaxation.

Spice It Up: The intimacy of a massage naturally leads to a deeper connection. If you're both comfortable, explore ways to increase the massage's sensuality. Use a feather or soft cloth for a lighter touch between deeper pressure, or introduce a warmed massage oil for a soothing feel. Trust your instincts and your partner's feedback to create a unique experience that feels special to both of you.

Pamper Your Partner

This evening is about giving to your partner without expecting anything in return. Focus on their relaxation and enjoyment. Encourage them to breathe deeply and let go of the day's stress while you focus on providing comfort and care through your touch. Massage benefits go beyond the physical—it's a way to communicate without words, expressing affection, trust, and appreciation.

If you want to make your partner feel cherished, offer to let them take the reins another night. This allows you to enjoy the experience fully without feeling rushed or obligated to reciprocate immediately.

Make It Last

After the massage, you can extend the relaxation by soaking in a warm bath together, wrapping up in soft blankets, and continuing the evening with a movie, quiet conversation, or simply cuddling. The connection doesn't have to end when the massage does—let the feeling of togetherness carry on throughout the night.

Conversation Starters

To deepen the emotional connection, consider engaging in some meaningful conversation during or after the massage:

- What is the most stressful part of your day-to-day life?
- How can I help you manage that stress?
- What's your favorite way to relax when you have some free time?
- What can I do to help you feel more cared for daily?

Taking the time to listen and respond to these questions can strengthen your bond, making you feel closer and more in tune with each other's needs. With the right ambiance, thoughtful touches, and a focus on pampering, the Soothe & Spoil Massage can become a go-to ritual for deepening intimacy and creating cherished memories together.

Terrarium

Creating a terrarium together can be more than just assembling a miniature garden; it's a fun way to connect, laugh, and see how your relationship can thrive like the little plants you're about to grow. Just as a terrarium needs the right balance of soil, light, and care, relationships benefit from attention, shared activities, and nurturing moments. Think of this project as a chance to create a living reminder of your love—a tiny world you build together.

What You'll Need

- Gravel
- Sheet Moss
- Terrarium Soil
- Succulents or small plants
- A Glass Terrarium or Bowl
- Decorative Pebbles or Figurines (optional)

Directions

Select Your Glass Container: Start by choosing a container that speaks to both of you. Do you prefer a rounded bowl that suggests harmony or a more angular, edgy shape that shows your unique personality? As long as it's deep enough for layers of gravel, moss, and soil, it's perfect. You can find terrarium kits with all the essentials or go on a shopping adventure to pick out your supplies.

Layer It Up: Pour a two-inch layer of gravel into the container. This will act as a drainage layer for your terrarium. If you want to add a personal touch, mix in a few colored stones or shells with sentimental meaning.

Add Sheet Moss: Next, lay down a layer of sheet moss to prevent the soil from slipping into the gravel. This gives the terrarium a lush, earthy appearance that sets the stage for the plants.

Terrarium Soil Time: Pour in the soil, spreading it out evenly. The amount of soil depends on the size of your plants. You'll want enough depth for the roots to settle in comfortably.

Plant Your Succulents or Mini Plants: Gently press your plants into the soil, arranging them in a way that looks good to both of you. Don't be afraid to get a little messy! If you're unsure which plants to choose, succulents are a safe bet because they're resilient and require minimal watering. However, if you prefer a more forest-like feel, tiny ferns and moss can make your terrarium look like a woodland hideaway.

Decorate and Enjoy: Sprinkle some decorative pebbles around the plants, or add a small figurine to represent a shared interest—a little reminder of this moment.

Spice It Up

Now that your hands are covered in soil and you've managed to scatter gravel all over the table, it's time for some playful cleaning up! Take turns washing each other's hands at the sink or share a steamy shower to clean up together. Make it a fun, bubbly experience—consider it part of the bonding ritual. After all, a little dirt never hurt anyone, but it sure can lead to some clean fun.

Terrarium Tips

This activity doesn't end with the initial planting! Make it a ritual to check in on your terrarium's progress together. Maybe once a week, see how the plants are doing and discuss any changes. Are they thriving, struggling, or slowly taking over the container? Use these moments to discuss your relationship as well—are there any areas that need more attention or a little extra love? Like the terrarium, your relationship will grow stronger with care.

Conversation Starters

- What's the most adventurous thing you've ever done with a partner?
- Do you think you have a green thumb or more of a 'plant killer' vibe?
- If you could plant a garden anywhere in the world, where would it be?
- How do you think people 'grow together' in relationships?

As the terrarium grows, it becomes a living symbol of your bond. You'll watch your tiny world flourish—or perhaps struggle a bit—just like every couple occasionally does. Whether your plants end up lush and green or a little wilted around the edges, remember that creating something together is what counts.

Romantic Inspiration

A timeless reminder for our modern hearts—*Elizabeth and Robert Browning's* love story shows us that true love laughs in the face of convention, even when life throws its biggest challenges our way. Whether it's age, illness, or an overbearing family, their passion inspired them to break free and live for what mattered most—each other. As I dove into their letters, I couldn't help but think times may change, but love's hurdles remain the same! So, take a note from history's most iconic romance and chase your dreams and passion—because a love that defies the odds is one worth holding onto. Here is a little taste of Elizabeth and Robert's romantic tale.

The love story of Elizabeth Barrett Browning and Robert Browning was as remarkable as it was unconventional. At a time when age differences, fragile health, and family control could easily stand in the way of true love, their bond defied the expectations of Victorian society. Six years older and long confined to her home due to chronic illness, Elizabeth found herself the object of Robert's deep admiration. Though many saw her as too frail for marriage, Robert's love transcended societal norms. Through their passionate letters, he pursued her heart, undeterred by the physical or social barriers they faced. Their intellectual connection only fueled the romance, with both poets finding solace, inspiration, and a shared creative brilliance in one another.

But theirs was also a love forged in secrecy and rebellion. Elizabeth's overbearing father, who forbade his children from marrying, was a looming force over her life. Yet, when Robert entered her world, he brought with him the possibility of freedom and independence. Their courtship, filled with letters of longing and devotion, culminated in an elopement that broke the chains of her father's control. The couple left England and began a new life together in

Italy, their love flourishing despite the circumstances that sought to keep them apart. In their letters, Elizabeth's words reveal a heart transformed by the courage and tenderness of a love that defied convention, while Robert's unwavering devotion lit a path toward liberation.

Elizabeth Barrett Browning to Robert Browning, 1845:

"I love your letters, dearest, beyond all love's speech and the writers' power, and think of you all day long... my thoughts flying to you as doves to their windows. I thank you, beloved, for all your tenderness—for every word, for every look. You have been far too good to me, too good. Can I ever make up to you by any good or by my truest love? Will it be my sweet work always to try?"

Robert Browning to Elizabeth Barrett Browning, 1846"

"I look back, and in every one point, every moment of our relation, I see you have been entirely my blessing and good. I have done nothing at all for you. ... My life is in you; your life has shown me my true self, and that self, I see, was worth finding."

Signature Cocktail

Turn cocktail-making into a fun and flirty evening with your partner by crafting a signature drink that captures your tastes. Mixing drinks is more than just pouring spirits into a glass; it's a way to connect, be playful, and share a memorable experience. Your mission: create a delicious drink that reflects your relationship—sweet, sour, bold, or even slightly spicy. As you craft your cocktail, you'll make more than just a drink; you'll create a memory.

What You'll Need

Ingredients

- **Spirits**: Vodka, gin, rum, tequila, whiskey, or whatever base liquor you both enjoy.
- **Mixers**: Soda water, tonic water, ginger beer, or flavored seltzers.
- **Fresh Juices**: Lemon, lime, orange, or pineapple for a burst of acidity.
- **Sweeteners**: Simple syrup, honey, agave, or a flavored syrup for added sweetness.
- **Bitters**: Add a few dashes to bring depth and complexity; many varieties exist.
- **Garnishes and Herbs**: Fresh fruit slices, mint, basil, or rosemary for that final touch.

Tools

- You will need a cocktail shaker, muddler, jigger (or measuring spoon), strainer, bar spoon, and a cutting board with a knife. If you want to get fancy, you can look for vintage barware or quirky glasses that make the experience even more special.

Directions

Set the Scene: Start by creating a mood with an inspiring playlist you love—something upbeat, jazzy, or romantic, depending on your mood. Lay out your ingredients and tools so everything is within reach.

Discuss Your Flavor Preferences: Before you begin, discuss what drinks you enjoy. Do you prefer a crisp, refreshing taste or something rich and warm? This helps you narrow the options and focus on a base spirit that appeals to you both.

Start Mixing: Start with your chosen spirit as the foundation. Then, add ingredients in small amounts, starting with fresh juices and sweeteners. Use a muddler to press herbs or fruit to release their flavors gently. Add a few dashes of bitters if you like a hint of complexity. Mix it up, sip, and adjust until the flavors are just right.

Balance is Key: A good cocktail has a harmonious blend of sweet, sour, bitter, and alcohol. If the drink tastes too sharp, add a touch of sweetness; if it's too sweet, a squeeze of citrus juice will balance it out.

Get Creative: Don't hesitate to experiment with unusual combinations. Maybe a splash of ginger beer and a dash of cinnamon will give your drink an unexpected twist, or a slice of cucumber and some elderflower liqueur will take it in a refreshing direction.

Give It a Name: Once you've fine-tuned the recipe, christen your creation with a meaningful name for both of you. Whether it's a blend of your names or inspired by an inside joke, naming the drink is part of making it truly yours.

Spice It Up

Treat yourselves to some fun or unique bar tools and glassware for an added element of fun. A fancy shaker or trendy cocktail glasses can make the experience feel like a special event. For a playful touch, you could even add some cocktail umbrellas, swizzle sticks, or colored straws. If you're feeling adventurous, try a themed night: tiki bar vibes, speakeasy-style, or a tropical escape.

Take It up a Notch

Make it a social activity by inviting friends for a cocktail competition, where each couple crafts a unique drink and shares the recipe. Let the group vote on the best-tasting cocktail, and the winners can enjoy bragging rights.

Conversation Starters

To keep the night flowing, here are some cocktail-themed questions to spark conversation and laughter:

- What was the first drink you ever had? Did you love it or hate it?
- What would it be if you could only drink one cocktail for the rest of your life?
- What's the worst cocktail you've ever tried, and what made it so terrible?
- If you could invent a drink named after you, what would it be like?

Why It's Worth It

Crafting a signature cocktail is more than just mixing drinks; it's about blending your unique tastes and discovering how two different flavors can complement each other. It's a reminder that working together can create something unique in a glass or life. The drink you create symbolizes your relationship—perfectly imperfect and constantly evolving. Cheers to love and creativity!

Vision Board

Creating a vision board as a couple is a fun and inspiring way to explore your shared dreams, ambitions, and desires. This activity goes beyond gluing magazine cutouts onto a poster board; it's about connecting on a whole new level. When you create something together, you get a sneak peek into each other's hearts and minds, sparking discussions that bring you closer and build trust.

What you'll need

- **A large poster board** – to serve as the canvas for your dreams.
- **Crafting supplies: Gather markers, scissors, magazines, glitter, construction paper, stickers, glue sticks, and anything else that will** make your board pop.

Directions

Set the Scene: Grab some comfy pillows, put on your favorite playlist, and settle down with your supplies. This should be a relaxed, distraction-free zone where you can laugh, chat, and dream.

Talk About Your Future: Discuss what you envision for your future. Where do you see yourselves in five years? Ten? Are there specific goals you aim for together, like traveling, building a dream home, or working towards a healthier lifestyle? Talking about the future can energize and help you understand each other's ambitions.

List Your Goals and Dreams: Write down a few goals and dreams you want to work on together. Make them specific and personal—the more detailed, the better. Your dream could be anything from owning a cozy mountain cabin to running a marathon. You'll turn your dreams into tangible, achievable goals by visualizing them.

Get Crafty: Now comes the fun part. Cut out magazine photos, print images, or sketch your ideas to represent each goal visually. If you dream of that big yard, find a picture of a beautiful garden. Are you thinking about financial stability? Glue on images of piggy banks or dollar signs. Are you dreaming of health and fitness? Draw weights, running shoes, or healthy meals. Use bright colors, add inspiring words or quotes, and let your board reflect your shared vision.

Wrap it Up Together: Once your vision board is complete, step back and admire your work. You're not just looking at pieces of paper glued to a board—you're looking at the life you both want to build. Display it somewhere you can see it regularly as a reminder of your shared dreams and journey together.

Spice It Up

After crafting the big dreams for your life together, it's time to add a little twist. Grab some paper, markers, and a sprinkle of glitter, and create a mini "vision" for your next 30 minutes. It could be anything fun, like drawing your partner a roadmap to your favorite date idea or adding sparkly arrows pointing to "silly dance time" in the living room. These little touches lighten the mood and make the experience even more memorable.

Conversation Starters

If you're unsure where to start or need some prompts to keep the ideas flowing, try these:

- *"Where do you see us in five years? Ten? Fifty?"*
- *"What are your biggest dreams for us?"*
- *"What's one thing you're most grateful for in our relationship right now?"*

Creating a vision board together encourages you to envision the best possible future, and as Helen Keller once said, *"The only thing worse than being blind is having sight, but no vision."*

Sunrise Yoga & Brunch

What You'll Need

- A yoga class or video to guide you both through some gentle morning stretches
- A peaceful spot to watch the sunrise — think beach, park, or hillside
- Yoga mats
- Optional: yoga blocks for extra support
- Picnic brunch goodies

Directions

To start, pick a yoga video or class that feels right for both of you — something calming to match the tranquility of dawn. Pack your mats and any other items you might need. Head to your chosen spot, making sure to arrive just before sunrise. Set up, lie back, and watch the sky shift from dark to light as you two prepare to flow through your movements.

Begin the yoga session with gentle, slow stretches to warm your muscles. Use each inhale to feel the peace around you and each exhale to let go of tension. As the sunlight filters in, let it energize you. Move through poses that bring you closer, like a seated forward fold where you can support each other or simple breathing exercises together.

Afterward, enjoy the picnic you've prepared! It doesn't have to be fancy, just a mix of your favorite brunch treats. Try something fun and a little indulgent, like chicken and waffles or a variety of mini pastries. You could also keep it light with fresh fruit, yogurt, nuts, and cheeses. Don't forget the mimosas; or if you'd like, a fresh juice blend to match the mood.

Spice It Up

Looking to elevate the experience? Try a few poses from partner yoga! AcroYoga can be a fun way to build trust and balance. Hold each other's weight as you move through a few playful lifts or balancing postures. It adds an element of teamwork and physical closeness, reminding you of the support you provide one another in daily life.

If you want to keep things spontaneous, finish the morning with a cozy breakfast at home. You can take turns cooking together or surprise each other with a favorite dish. A yoga session often brings peace and presence, and breakfast in bed could add some unexpected romance to the day.

Conversation Starters

To bring in some meaningful conversation during or after brunch, try these questions to deepen your connection:

- *What's a small moment that made you happy this week?*
- *If you could live anywhere in the world for a month, where would it be?*
- *What's one thing about our relationship that you value?*

By incorporating these light-hearted yet meaningful questions, you cflect on each other's lives and dreams. The best part about Sunrise Yoga & Brunch is that it's all about togetherness — whether you're holding hands, sharing a laugh over a clumsy AcroYoga attempt, or quietly soaking up the sunrise. Make it a ritual that reminds you of how nice it is to be in each other's presence.

Geocaching

What You'll Need

- The Geocaching App
- **Comfortable Clothes and Shoes** - Think like an adventurer, ready for rugged paths or city parks.
- **Easy Snacks** - Pack something simple, or plan to grab a treat along the way.
- **Camera or Smartphone** - Capture those exciting finds and document your discoveries in the app.

Directions

Start by downloading the Geocaching app and looking for nearby geocaches (or venture out to more distant spots if you're both up for a road trip). The app is your guide, giving you all the hints and coordinates needed to locate the hidden geocaches. Once you reach a location, the real fun begins. Geocaches are often hidden in plain sight but are cleverly camouflaged, so you'll need to work together, using sharp observation skills and creative problem-solving to find each cache.

Some caches contain fun items for trading or tracking—an added layer of mystery! After you find a cache, remember to sign its logbook and document your adventure in the app, leaving a piece of your journey behind for future explorers. This experience is about collaboration, communication, and sharing moments that are both challenging and joyful.

What is Geocaching?

Geocaching is the world's most giant treasure-hunting game, with over 3 million hidden geocaches waiting to be found across the globe. Every geocache holds a unique story and a chance to step into a worldwide community of explorers, sharing in the thrill of discovery. From urban parks to remote trails, geocaching encourages you to explore new places and make lasting memories.

Why Geocaching is Perfect for Couples

There's something extraordinary about embarking on an adventure with your partner, especially one that requires teamwork and problem-solving. Geocaching encourages you to step outside your routine, explore new places, and share the excitement of discovery. Whether you're deciphering clues, navigating unfamiliar paths, or celebrating a successful find, the experience fosters connection and laughter. It's an opportunity to see each other's playful, adventurous side and to cheer each other on through the process.

Conversation Starters

- *What do you treasure most in life?*
- *Would you consider yourself adventurous? Why, or why not?*
- *What's something you'd love to discover in a geocache?*

A Love Story to Inspire Your Adventure

Jenny and Kevin stood together at the edge of a cliff, overlooking a canyon where a river roared below. The harness dug into Jenny's shoulders as she triple-checked it, while Kevin stood beside her, cool as ever, his blue eyes gleaming with excitement.

"Ready?" he asked, reaching for her hand.

Jenny's heart raced. Sure, she wanted an adventure, but zip-lining over a canyon? She wasn't sure she could do it. With Kevin squeezing her hand, though, she felt a surge of courage. Taking a deep breath, she glanced at him, her nerves transforming into a competitive spark. "Ladies first?" he grinned.

"Just watch me," she replied, raising her chin.

"Believe me, I will," he laughed, his voice steady.

With one last deep breath, Jenny leaped. The wind whipped past her face, the world a blur of trees and water below. She let out a wild laugh, heart pounding with excitement and joy. Glancing back, she caught a glimpse of Kevin's expression as he watched her—half in awe, half amusement. They locked eyes, and for a second, everything else faded away. This was their moment.

When her feet finally touched the ground, she turned, arms raised in triumph. Kevin landed moments later, pulling her into a hug as they laughed. In that single, fearless moment, she'd found something extraordinary—how incredible life could be when they took on challenges together.

Whether it's leaping off a cliff or just finding a quiet place to watch the stars, the experience will stay with you, a reminder of what you can accomplish together. Your outdoor adventure doesn't have to be extreme—what matters is that you try something new, face any fears, and support each other all along the way. And when you look back, you'll both have a unique story that belongs only to you two— a moment in time when you took a leap, held each other's hands, and discovered a new side of your love.

Outdoor Adventure

Spending time outdoors brings couples closer by creating lasting memories, strengthening trust, and sparking laughter in new, shared experiences. While taking on an outdoor adventure may sound intimidating, that's part of the fun! When you and your partner step out of your comfort zones together, you'll likely enjoy the exhilaration and laughter of trying something new.

What You'll Need

- **Essentials** like a solid plan and a willingness to step out of your comfort zone.
- **Specialty equipment** depending on the activity. For instance:
  - **Fishing or Canoeing**: Fishing poles, bait, life jackets, or paddles.
  - **Hiking or Camping**: Durable boots, a tent, snacks, and water.
  - **Extreme Activities**: Gear suited for bungee jumping, zip-lining, or scuba diving (rented or borrowed).
- **A sense of adventure** – whether you're doing something mild or heart-pounding, bring excitement and open-mindedness along for the ride!

Getting Started: Choosing the Adventure

Begin by discussing what sounds exciting with each other. Adventure ideas can range from the thrill of skydiving to the tranquility of camping. Here are some ideas:

- **Sky Diving**: Jump out of a plane and watch the ground rush up to meet you (a bucket-list experience for thrill-seekers!).
- **White-Water Rafting**: Tackle rushing rapids and soak up the wild energy of nature.
- **Hiking or Camping**: Explore scenic trails and pitch a tent under the stars.
- **Rock Climbing**: Work together to scale new heights and enjoy stunning views.
- **Zip Lining**: Glide through forests and valleys, taking in nature from above.
- **Surfing**: Get a crash course in balance and let the waves carry you both toward shore.
- **Fishing or Canoeing**: Embrace a quieter adventure, paddling along serene rivers or casting lines at sunrise.
- **Skiing or Snowboarding**: Take on snowy slopes and enjoy the crisp winter air.

Spicing It Up: Planning an Overnight Adventure

To make it more memorable, consider booking a unique overnight stay. Try a weekend getaway to a cozy treehouse retreat or a rustic mountain cabin. Imagine waking up to birdsong, sharing coffee as the morning mist lifts, or cozying up by a fireplace after a day on the slopes. Just a night or two away from routine can deepen the experience and leave you both with plenty to discuss.

Step By Step Directions

Pick an Adventure Together: Whether it's a daring cliff dive or a peaceful nature hike, choose something that interests both of you. Challenge yourselves to try something you've never done before!

Get the Gear You Need: Gather all the equipment, research your destination, and dress for the weather. Don't forget to pack snacks, water, and a camera to capture the highlights.

Prepare Mentally: Nervous? That's normal! A little pep talk or motivational podcast can boost confidence before trying something new.

Support Each Other: This experience is about connection. Hold hands, laugh through moments of hesitation, and encourage each other to take that leap (metaphorical or literal). Remember, it's not about perfection—it's about creating memories together.

Reflect on the Experience: Share your favorite moments and what you learned after your adventure. Reliving the experience through each other's perspective will make it even more memorable.

Conversation Starters

- **"What is the craziest thing you've ever done?"** Sharing past adventures (and mishaps) will likely lead to some laughs and a deeper connection.

- **"How did that work out for you?"** Talking about those moments can bring back memories of courage, fun, or even the hilarious missteps that make great stories.

- **"What's the craziest thing on your bucket list?"** Dreaming together is one way to get to know each other better. Who knows? Maybe your partner has been itching to try something wild and adventurous!

As motivational author Neale Donald Walsch said, "Life begins at the end of your comfort zone." Venturing into the unknown with someone you love is a great way to expand your horizons together and strengthen your bond.

City Walk

What You'll Need

- Just curiosity and a positive attitude.

Directions

Head out to the nearest city or town and let your journey unfold. Whether walking, driving, or taking the bus, your goal is to explore together. Plan a route, if necessary, but allow some spontaneity—venturing into shops, cafes, bookstores, parks, or maybe even that intriguing alley you've always wondered about.

Experiencing a place on foot allows you to engage with your surroundings in new ways. You'll discover hidden gems: quiet coffee spots, cozy book nooks, or unique boutiques. Moving slowly, with each other for company, makes this more than just a walk.

You'll notice the details—a mural on a corner building, the scent from a bakery, the chatter of street musicians—that create a place's character. You'll build memories and open fresh perspectives by pausing to explore and experience the city through a shared lens.

Spice It Up: The Date with New Eyes

To give your city walk a twist, dress up and pretend it's your first date. Walk through the streets as if you're still learning about each other, exploring the city and your partner's thoughts and perspectives on it. Take turns guiding each other to favorite places or spots that spark curiosity.

Let your partner give you a "tour" as if they're seeing everything for the first time. Ask questions, learn what they love, and share stories. The goal is to view each other with fresh eyes, deepen your bond, and let the city be the canvas for your shared adventure.

The Art of Wandering: Finding Hidden Gems Together

One of the joys of a city walk is the unpredictability. Turn down an unfamiliar street or pop into a quirky storefront—who knows what you'll find? Whether you stumble upon a quiet gallery, or a cozy park bench perfect for people-watching, the little surprises make this exploration memorable.

Maybe you'll find a new favorite café or perhaps a thrift store filled with old records that spark a wave of nostalgia. The key is to be open to the unknown, letting curiosity guide you. These moments of discovery can spark new interests, inside jokes, or shared moments of wonder that add new dimensions to your relationship.

Conversation Starters

To keep the conversation flowing, try these prompts:

- *What's the most fun date we've ever had, and why was it special?*
- *Are you someone who loves spontaneity, or do you prefer to have a plan?*
- *What's something new you'd love to try together?*

These questions bring lighthearted and reflective elements to your outing, helping you learn more about each other's personalities, preferences, and dreams.

Portraits of the Heart

What You'll Need

- Drawing paper
- Your choice of drawing medium: pencils, charcoal, pastels, paints, markers
- Props for creating the perfect portrait (optional: chair, sofa, blankets, costumes, or themed items)

Directions

Start by deciding who will be the artist and who will be the model. While one of you gets to play the muse, the other takes on the artist's role—but don't worry, there's no pressure to be Picasso! Set a playful tone and establish a time limit, perhaps 10 or 20 minutes, so neither of you feels pressure to create a masterpiece. The goal isn't perfection; it's about building something meaningful (and maybe a little hilarious!) together.

Let the model settle into a comfortable spot, and if you're feeling adventurous, add props or a theme. Decide on the vibe—will this be a casual pose or something more daring? Feel free to try a whimsical or playful approach, adding touches that make each portrait as unique as your relationship. Throughout the session, don't stop laughing together, sharing little comments, or breaking into exaggerated poses to make each other smile.

As the artist, take the time to appreciate every detail of your partner's face, expression, and posture. This isn't just about drawing but about studying your partner and maybe noticing new little things—their smile lines, relaxed posture, or even their laughter as you struggle to capture them on paper.

Spice it Up: Try switching roles or adding a unique theme—dress in costumes, channeling your favorite movie characters or historical figures. Or, if you're both feeling bold, try a more relaxed, vulnerable approach. Remember, being playful and vulnerable together strengthens your bond and keeps things lighthearted and fun.

Figure Drawing – A Fresh Take on Your Partner

In traditional art circles, figure drawing is a profound practice, but here, it's an opportunity to look at your partner with fresh eyes. This exercise lets you observe each other deeply, studying the details that sometimes go unnoticed. Notice the curve of their smile, how their hair frames their face, or the expression in their eyes. It's a chance to appreciate your partner's unique features, quirks, and expressions.

No matter how the artwork turns out, share the compliments that come to mind as you sketch. Tell them when something catches your eye—whether it's the gentle curve of their jaw or how they laugh at your attempt to capture their likeness. These moments make it a bonding experience that's as romantic as it is fun.

Conversation Starters

- Have you ever taken an art class?
- Would you be interested in taking one together?
- If you could master any art style, what would it be?
- Is there an art piece that has always moved you?

Bonus: Inspiration from Rose Dewitt-Bukater, Titanic's Famous Muse: "Draw me like one of your French girls." This playful nod to the famous line from *Titanic* sets the stage for an adventurous, lighthearted session. Try to embody the spirit of classic muses, adding a touch of romance, a bit of humor, and plenty of charm.

After your drawing session, share your artwork. Reflect on the experience, appreciating the beauty in the imperfections and celebrating the connection it brought. Frame your favorite pieces or keep them tucked away as a memory of this creative moment together. Whether you end up with cherished keepsakes or comical attempts, the real art will be the memories you've created as a couple.

Ten Things

What You'll Need

- A piece of paper and a pen for each of you
- A ten-minute timer

Directions

Set the timer and list ten things you genuinely love about your partner each time. No peeking or sharing what you've written down yet!

Once time's up, get ready to act it out! Take turns choosing one thing from your list and acting it out charades-style while your partner tries to guess what you're expressing.

After taking two or three turns, tally up the correct guesses. Whoever guessed the most wins!

As a bonus, come up with a fun reward for the winner—maybe they can choose the next date night activity or home-cooked meal!

Spice it Up

Want to take things to the next level? Instead of listing the things you love about each other, write down ten things you'd love to do *with* your partner — think romantic, playful, or flirty. Act these out, too, and then see where your lists overlap for instant new date ideas!

Making the Most of the "Ten Things" Game

This activity is a fantastic way to reconnect with each other and make your partner feel genuinely seen and valued. If "words of affirmation" are a big part of how you feel love, this is a great chance to show it — but with a twist! Acting it out instead of saying it directly keeps it light and fun, giving you both the thrill of a guessing game while still hearing the things you cherish most. This activity can bring laughter, warmth, and maybe even a little spark if you try the spicy version!

Conversation Starters

To keep the connection going after the game, try asking each other:

- *"What did you think I would say I love most about you?"*
- *"Why do you think [insert your favorite quality here] is my favorite thing about you?"*

Enjoy deepening your bond and having some good laughs along the way. Let this be a reminder that the most straightforward words and gestures can be the most powerful.

Two Truths and a Lie

What You'll Need
- A piece of paper and a pen.
- Your best poker face.

Directions

Each partner writes down three statements about themselves. Ensure that two statements are bizarre yet true and the third is a complete fabrication.

Exchange lists with your partner and take turns guessing which statement is the lie.

After revealing the truth, discuss the stories behind each true statement, diving into the details that make your lives unique. Repeat for as many rounds as you like; the possibilities are endless!

Example Statements
- *I once had dinner with a famous author.*
- *I've never broken a bone in my body.*
- *I can do an impressive impersonation of a chicken.*

The fun of this game lies in its unpredictability. You might think you know everything about your partner, but this game will surprise you! For instance, your partner once participated in a local talent show that you had no idea about. Or perhaps they have a hidden talent, like juggling or solving a Rubik's cube in under a minute. These revelations spark laughter, storytelling, and a deeper understanding of each other's past experiences and personalities.

Spice It Up

To add a little thrill, introduce playful consequences. For each correct guess, the winner can request the loser to remove an article of clothing (keeping it light-hearted and fun!) If a partner guesses incorrectly, they might have to take a tequila shot or share an embarrassing story from their past; this not only makes the game more exciting but also creates a relaxed atmosphere where both partners can laugh off mistakes and enjoy each other's company.

Additional Conversation Starters

- What is something I know about you that no one else knows?
- How well do you think you know me?
- If you could relive one moment in your life, what would it be and why?
- What is your most unusual talent that I might not know about?

This game encourages open dialogue, strengthens your connection, and creates fun banter opportunities. You'll learn unexpected facts about each other and discover the joy of shared laughter and playful competition. So grab your pens and get ready for a night of surprises, laughter, and deeper intimacy!

Cultural Cuisine

What You'll Need

- A new recipe and all the ingredients that go along with it.
- Cultural music sets the mood.
- Optional: Cultural decorations and clothing to enhance the experience.

Directions

Start your adventure by choosing a state or country you'd like to explore together. This could be a place you've always wanted to visit or somewhere you know little about. Once you've picked your destination, find a traditional recipe representing that culture. This could be anything from Italian risotto to Japanese sushi or even a hearty German bratwurst. The key is to pick something that excites both of you!

Next, plan a trip to your local specialty food store. This is where the fun begins! As you gather your ingredients, take a moment to explore the aisles together. You might stumble upon unique spices, specialty sauces, or exotic fruits that could spark your culinary creativity. Don't forget to engage with the shop staff—they might offer tips or insights about the ingredients, enriching your experience.

Once you've gathered everything, return home to transform your kitchen into a culinary hotspot. Before you start cooking, create music that reflects the culture you're exploring. Imagine you're in a bustling market in Mexico with mariachi music playing or at an

Italian café with the sweet sounds of Pavarotti in the background. This will help transport you to your chosen destination, making the evening feel more special.

Now, for the cooking! As you prepare the dish, work together, share tasks, and enjoy each other's company. Cooking is a fantastic way to bond, and you can sneak in playful banter as you chop, stir, and taste. If you feel adventurous, consider dressing in cultural attire or decorating your dining space to mirror your destination. It can be as simple as a colorful tablecloth or as elaborate as themed dinnerware.

Spice It Up

For dessert, take it to the next level with a fun and interactive chocolate or honey drizzle. Set up a dessert station with fresh fruits, cakes, or pastries, and let your creativity flow. Dip strawberries in melted chocolate or drizzle honey over your favorite pastry. Pro tip: Remember to have a clean-up plan; kitchen tables are far easier to clean than bedrooms!

Why This Works?

This date night idea allows you to escape the ordinary and immerse yourself in another culture without leaving home. It's a fantastic way to learn about each other's tastes and preferences while creating memories. Plus, it opens the door for conversations that can deepen your connection.

Conversation Starters

To keep the conversation lively while you cook and dine, consider these questions:

- What is the weirdest food you've ever eaten, and what did you think of it?

- If you could travel anywhere in the world, where would you go, and why?
- What cultural cuisine have you always wanted to try?
- How do you think travel influences our understanding of different cultures?

This "Cultural Cuisine" date is not just about cooking; it's about creating a shared experience that sparks laughter, exploration, and connection. So gather your ingredients, set the stage, and get ready for a memorable night of fun and discovery!

Dance, Dance

What You'll Need

- Virtual classes or an instructional video online.
- Your best clothes, the ones that make you feel fabulous.
- A cozy living room or any space that feels special.
- Optional: fairy lights or candles for ambiance.

Directions

Start by donning outfits that make you feel confident and sexy. Think of this as your chance to shine—choose something that showcases your personality and boosts your self-esteem. Once you're dressed to impress, pick a virtual dance class or an instructional video that excites you. Transform your living room into a private dance studio, complete with an inviting atmosphere.

You can waltz gracefully across the floor, break out some hip-hop moves, or even learn a number from your favorite musical. Feeling adventurous? Aim for the iconic lift from *Dirty Dancing*—bonus points if you can nail it! Remember, this is about having fun together, so don't stress about perfection.

Spice it Up

To turn up the heat, dim the lights and light some candles to create a romantic vibe. For an extra twist, why not learn a sultry tango? Picture yourselves as passionate dancers, lost in the moment, and add a little flair by placing a de-thorned rose between your teeth. This not only adds humor but also encourages a playful atmosphere.

Why Dance?

Dancing is more than just moving your body to the beat; it's an intimate experience that helps build a connection. When you dance, you share a rhythm, and laughter often follows as you navigate new steps together. Music has a unique way of weaving memories, so don't worry if you have two left feet—just be sure to stumble into each other's arms when you trip up.

Conversation Starters

As you dance, let the music inspire your conversation. Here are some prompts to help you connect further:

- Did you attend your high school prom? What was that experience like?
- Who was your date, and what did you wear?
- How did it feel to dance with them?
- What's your favorite song to dance to and why?

Dance Toward A Love Connection

As you dance, share stories from your past, like this one:

Michael's hands trembled as he struggled to fasten the corsage onto Sofia's wrist. She looked stunning in her black-and-white rose-print gown, and they stood together in a bustling gymnasium adorned with twinkling lights and colorful decorations. The bass from the music thumped loudly, creating an electric atmosphere.

When the upbeat tune faded, a soft acoustic guitar filled the air, prompting Michael to ask Sofia for a dance. Nervously, they held each other at arm's length, both having never been on a date before. Although they really liked each other, their shyness created an awkwardness that hung in the air. Deciding to leave early, they ventured out into the parking lot, where a light mist began to fall, dampening their hair and making the moment feel even more intimate.

As Michael cranked the engine of his old blue pickup, a romantic song played on the radio—a man requesting "It's Your Love" by Tim McGraw for his wife on their anniversary. Inspired by the moment, Michael mustered his courage and asked Sofia for one last dance. She agreed, slipping off her heels and stepping down from the truck, her heart racing with excitement.

They swayed side to side in the rain, the world fading away around them. With a nervous smile, Sofia rested her head against Michael's chest. He placed his head atop hers, inhaling deeply, feeling a mix of relief and joy. They shared that magical dance in the rainy parking lot, completely lost in each other. Years later, they danced to that same song on their wedding day, a testament to their enduring love and the memories they created together.

Wrap Up

As your dance night ends, take a moment to reflect on the experience. Discuss what you loved about the dance, what was funny, and any moments that surprised you. This exercise not only brings you closer but also allows you to appreciate the lightheartedness and intimacy that dancing together can foster.

Dancing isn't just about the steps; it's about the connection, laughter, and memories you create together. So, put on your dancing shoes, let loose, and enjoy a night filled with joy, laughter, and love. This expanded idea focuses on making the experience more engaging and memorable while also enhancing the romantic and fun aspects of the dance. Let me know if you need any more adjustments!

Strip Jenga

What You'll Need

- A Jenga set (the more colorful, the better!)
- A whiteboard to keep track of points (optional, but adds a competitive edge)
- A playful attitude and maybe a drink or two to loosen up!

Directions

Start by putting on something exciting that makes you feel good—think playful, flirty, or downright sexy! Once you're both feeling the vibe, set up your Jenga tower. The classic game rules apply: stack the blocks and take turns removing one without toppling the tower. But here's the twist: if the tower collapses on your turn, it's time to lose a piece of clothing!

As you play, the stakes rise, and so does the laughter. When one of you loses all your clothes, you've both won—after all, what's more fun than a bit of playful nudity?

Spice it Up

For added fun, consider creative distractions while your partner is taking their turn. Try whispering silly jokes, or playfully teasing them about their clothing choices. You could even use props, like a feather or a silk scarf, to create lighthearted distractions. The key is to keep the atmosphere fun and flirty.

Conversation Starters

To deepen your connection during the game, toss in some fun questions. Here are a few to get you started:

- *Which of us is more competitive?*
- *Did you play a lot of games growing up? What was your favorite?*
- *What's the craziest game you've ever played?*

Why Strip Jenga?

Strip Jenga isn't just a game; it's an opportunity to connect and create memories that you'll laugh about later. It's a fantastic way to break the ice, especially if you've been feeling a bit stuck in your routine. The combination of strategy and playful teasing invites spontaneity, making it a great way to learn more about each other's personalities and playful sides.

Playing a game like this allows you to explore competitiveness in a light-hearted way. You'll discover who takes risks and who plays it safe. The playful banter and light tension can spark conversations about childhood games, personal stories, and shared memories, leading to deeper intimacy.

Plus, you'll both have a blast! Whether you win or lose, you'll be sharing laughter and smiles, and maybe even a little more vulnerability. Strip Jenga is more than just a fun activity; it's an invitation to let loose, be silly, and connect in ways you may not have before. So grab that Jenga set, turn on some upbeat music, and prepare for an unforgettable evening that will leave you both feeling closer than ever.

This expanded version of Strip Jenga provides more context, emphasizes the game's playful nature, and invites couples to connect through conversation while they play. Would you like to add or change anything?

Candle Craft

What You'll Need

- Meltable wax and a stirring stick
- A heat-resistant container (think quirky mugs or elegant jars)
- Candle scent of your choice (from vanilla to exotic sandalwood)
- Candle wicks and wick holders
- Scissors
- Double boil setup (a pot and a cheap glass measuring cup work wonders)
- Colors and decorative elements (think glitter, dried flowers, or colored wax)

Directions

Set the Mood: Before heading out, create a cozy atmosphere at home. Light some existing candles, play soft music, or even prepare some snacks to enjoy while you craft. This will set the stage for a fun and relaxed date.

Craft Store Adventure: Head to your local craft store together. Use this time not only to gather supplies but also to explore different scents and colors. Challenge each other to pick a scent that reflects a memory or an inside joke. This trip is about enjoying each other's company and indulging in some lighthearted banter as you navigate the aisles.

Double Boiler Setup: Back home, set up your double boiler. Boil water in a pot and hang a glass measuring cup over it by the handle. As the wax melts, take turns stirring and watching it transform. Talk about how your favorite scents can change your mood or share a funny story about a time you had an unexpected smell experience.

Prepare Your Containers: While the wax is melting, trim your wicks and secure them in your containers with wick holders. For a fun twist, decorate your containers with paint or stickers that represent your relationship or even write little messages to each other on them. This adds a personal touch that makes the candles truly special.

Mixing Magic: Once the wax is fully melted, add the scent and optional colors. Stir them in together, making this a teamwork moment. You can share stories about why you chose each scent. Perhaps one reminds you of a vacation, or another brings to mind your first date.

Pour and Set: Carefully pour the scented wax into your containers, taking care not to spill (this is where the teamwork really counts!). As you wait for them to set, why not play a game? Try "20 Questions" or "Two Truths and a Lie" to keep the fun going.

The Grand Finale: Once the candles have set, it's time to light them up! Use this moment to share what you hope each candle represents in your relationship. Will it symbolize love friendship, or passion?

Spice it Up

- **Romantic Ambiance:** Light your candle during a romantic dinner at home to create a cozy atmosphere. Allow the scent to envelop you as you share a meal and connect.
- **Messages in Wax:** Write secret notes on the bottom of the containers before pouring in the wax. When the candle burns down, your partner will discover a hidden message that

brings back beautiful memories or sweet words of affirmation.

Conversation Starters

- What's a smell that brings back a cherished memory for you?
- If you could create a candle that represents our relationship, what scent would you choose and why?
- What's your favorite seasonal scent, and how does it make you feel?

Candle crafting isn't just about making candles; it's about creating memories, sharing laughs, and deepening your connection. Enjoy this aromatic journey together!

Steamy Messages

What You'll Need
- Rubbing alcohol
- Q-tips

Directions

Head to your bathroom with your supplies in hand. Dip a Q-tip into the rubbing alcohol, making sure it's just damp enough to draw but not so wet that it drips. This is key to keeping your secret message neat and tidy! With your partner's favorite phrase or a little love doodle in mind, write it out on the mirror. Try to be clever or funny—maybe draw a silly heart or write, "I love you, but don't forget to rinse!"

Now comes the fun part: the reveal! When your partner steps into the shower, the steam will begin to fog up the mirror. But surprise! The spots where you apply the rubbing alcohol will remain clear, unveiling your secret message. It's a delightful surprise that sets a romantic tone for the day or night ahead.

Spice It Up

This playful activity can easily be turned into a fun game! Challenge each other to write messages back and forth throughout the week. One day, leave a cheeky note that hints at a fun evening planned; the next, send a reminder of a cherished memory. For a twist, incorporate a little competition: see who can come up with the most creative message or drawing. The winner gets to choose the next date night activity!

Steamy Messages—A Flirty Tradition

This little ritual can add a dash of excitement to your daily routine. Imagine starting the day with a smile because your partner has left a sweet note just for you. Or how about a cheeky message to light up a mundane moment? You can even surprise them with an encouraging quote before a big meeting or a simple "You've got this!" before they head out.

Conversation Starters

This playful approach also opens the door to deeper conversations. As you share messages, discuss what made you choose certain phrases or drawings. Here are some starters to inspire a heartfelt chat:

- *What would you change about yourself, if you could?*
- *What do you like most about yourself?*
- *What do you like most about me?*

These light-hearted questions will encourage both of you to reflect and share, fostering a deeper connection.

"The world is filled with hidden love."—Daniella Kessler

Memory Box

What You'll Need

- A box: A sturdy cardboard box will do for keeping in your closet, but if you're feeling adventurous and want to bury it, opt for something waterproof.
- Paper and pen: Use decorative paper for added flair and to reflect your personality.
- Photographs, mementos, creative objects: Collect items that represent your relationship and shared experiences.

Directions

Get ready for a fun and heartfelt experience as you create a time capsule together! Start by setting aside an afternoon to focus solely on this project without distractions. Gather your supplies and find a cozy spot—maybe a café, your living room, or even a beautiful park.

Begin by discussing what you want to include in your memory box. This is your chance to reminisce and share stories about each item. Think of photographs from trips you've taken together, ticket stubs from concerts or movies, and other mementos that hold special meaning. You could even include little notes about why each item is significant.

Next, each of you should write a letter to the other. Reflect on your journey together so far and express your hopes and dreams for the future. This personal touch adds depth to the experience, making it even more meaningful. Seal the letters in an envelope and include them in the box.

Once you've gathered everything, put it all in the box and seal it up. Decide on an opening date—will it be one year, five years, or even ten years down the road? Write this date on the box as a reminder, and then hide it away in a special spot. If you choose to bury it, note the location so you can easily find it later.

Spice It Up

For an added element of surprise, consider writing a playful, romantic letter detailing a future date or trip. Don't let your partner read it until the day you reveal it. This build-up of excitement will create delightful anticipation that adds an extra layer of fun to the experience.

Make It a Tradition

Consider creating a memory box every year for your anniversary. As the years go by, you'll develop a beautiful collection of memories that capture the essence of your relationship. You'll be amazed at the things your partner chooses to include—and you might even rediscover memories you had forgotten about when you open the boxes in the future.

Conversation Starters

- *What is your favorite memory of us?*
- *What is a memory you would like for us to create in the future?*

As Winnie the Pooh wisely said, "We didn't realize we were making memories, we just knew we were having fun." Creating a memory box together is a wonderful way to intentionally make those memories while strengthening your bond. So grab your materials, get creative, and enjoy this journey of reflection and connection!

Breakfast in Bed

What You'll Need

- Ingredients for a stunning breakfast (think eggs, fresh fruit, pancakes, French toast, waffles, po enta, bacon, sausage, or oatmeal)
- A tray for serving
- A small vase with flowers
- Your partner's favorite coffee or tea, served just the way they like it
- A playful or sexy apron (optional)

Directions

Start the day with a beautiful gesture by surprising your partner with breakfast in bed! Quietly slip out of bed, so you don't wake them, and take your time to create something special. Choose foods you know they love, or try a new recipe together!

Try stacking pancakes or waffles for a whimsical look or going for something classic like eggs and toast with a colorful side of fresh berries. Presentation counts, so arrange everything with care on the tray, adding a flower in a vase for an extra touch. When you bring it to them, go the extra mile by setting it up comfortably for them to enjoy.

Spice it Up

Bring breakfast wearing only an apron, adding a playful twist they won't soon forget! Or consider adding a romantic playlist playing softly in the background to make it feel even more special.

Make it a Tradition

To capture the memories, take a picture of the breakfast setup each time you do this—over time, you'll have a collection of these morning moments to look back on. You can even turn it into an anniversary tradition, with a new breakfast-in-bed surprise each year.

Conversation Starters

To add some fun and get to know each other more, use these light breakfast-themed questions to spark conversation:

- What's your favorite breakfast fruit?
- What's one fruit you've never tried that you'd like to?
- Are you more of a full-breakfast person, or a grab-and-go kind of person?

This "recipe" will leave you both with a cozy morning filled with love, laughter, and maybe a little adventure!

Drury Lane

What You'll Need

- A muffin recipe and all the ingredients it calls for
- A comfortable pair of handcuffs (or a playful substitute like a scarf)

Directions

Gather your ingredients and set up your kitchen as a cozy baking station. Now, here's the twist: handcuff your dominant wrist to your partner's! This will require you to coordinate each step of the muffin-making process together. No cheating!

Measure and mix with careful collaboration—one person might hold the bowl while the other scoops the flour. Expect some mess and giggles as you try to whisk, stir, and pour while bound together!

Once the muffins are in the oven, take a little timeout to relax. Use the baking time to chat, dance, or just enjoy each other's company, still handcuffed if you're up for it.

When the muffins are done, savor the fruits of your labor together!

Spice It Up

Try adding an extra layer of fun by challenging each other with mini tasks while you're cuffed, like seeing if you can high-five with free hands or setting a playful goal like decorating the muffins without "uncuffing." If you're both up for it, you might even keep the cuffs on for your post-muffin plans!

Conversation Starters

- *What's one thing you think we could improve on as a team?*
- *Do you think we're good communicators? Why or why not?*
- *If we could work together on any project, big or small, what would you want it to be?*

Inspiration

Do you know the Muffin Man? Embrace the classic children's rhyme with a playful twist as you become your own "Drury Lane" bakers! This activity is all about getting closer, improving your teamwork, and—of course—enjoying a sweet treat together.

One Lucky Cookie

What You'll Need

- A tasty fortune cookie recipe (no worries, I've got one ready for you!)
- Oven
- Two different storage containers or bags (to keep things organized)
- Small slips of paper and pens for writing
- Optional: Your favorite Asian takeout (perfect for setting the mood!)

Directions

Prepping the Fortunes: Start by cutting small strips of paper for your messages. Get creative! Whether it's a heartfelt compliment, a funny inside joke, or a spicy secret, these notes are all about making your partner feel special and keeping the mystery alive.

Hide and Seek: Write your messages in secret so your partner doesn't see. Slip each note into a folded cookie dough round, then carefully shape the dough around it. If you're up for a little challenge, try shaping the fortune cookies together – the trick is to keep each other's notes hidden!

Bake and Separate: Once baked and cooled, store each batch separately so you know which cookies are which. Keep them in labeled containers so you won't be tempted to peek!

Surprise Over Time: This recipe should make about a dozen cookies, so you'll each get a nice little fortune from one another on more than one occasion. Scatter the fun throughout the week by exchanging a cookie or two each day!

Spice It Up

Want to keep the fun going? Leave hints or playful teases about what's coming up in their "fortunes." For example, "Tomorrow will bring laughter and a bit of mystery..." Or plan a surprise based on one of the fortunes!

One Lucky Cookie: Love is the Sweetest Fortune

Sharing a little sweetness in your day is such a simple way to connect. Plus, fortune cookies carry a bit of whimsy, hinting at the fun in your relationship. Who knew baking could bring you closer? Besides, with a little luck and a lot of love, your messages might just bring some delightful surprises.

Conversation Starters

- *What's something in life you feel incredibly lucky to have experienced?*
- *Do you think our meeting was fate, luck, or something else?*
- *If you could see into our future, what would you love to see there?*

This twist on fortune cookies adds a touch of suspense and warmth to your time together—enjoy your lucky moments!

Fortune Cookie Recipe

https://www.fifteenspatulas.com/fortune-cookies/

Ingredients

- 3 large egg whites
- 3/4 cup sugar
- 1/2 cup melted butter
- 1/4 tsp vanilla extract
- 1/4 tsp almond extract
- 3 tbsp water
- 1 cup all-purpose flour *(5 oz by weight)*

Preheat the oven to 375 degrees F. Line a sheet pan with parchment paper or a silicone mat and have your fortune strips ready to go.

- In a stand mixer (or large bowl with a hand mixer), whip the egg whites and sugar on high speed for about 2 minutes, until frothy. Whip in the melted butter, vanilla, almond extract, and water until incorporated. Add the flour and mix until the flour *just* disappears.

- With a tablespoon measure, spoon the batter onto the parchment paper and spread it out into an even 3-inch circle. I recommend not doing any more than 2-3 at a time, since they set very quickly, and you will not be able to fold more than that.

- Bake the fortune cookies for 7-8 minutes, until the edges brown slightly. If you let them brown too much, they will snap when you shape them. Conversely, if they don't brown a little bit, they will also break (but tear, rather than snap).

- When each batch of fortune cookies finishes baking, remove them from the oven and quickly flip the circle over, and fold your fortune cookie in half, into a semicircle. This is when you slip your note into the cookie (quickly) because if you slip it in right at the beginning, the cookie will be too hot, and your paper will stick to the cookie. Place your semicircle onto the edge of a cup, and quickly fold the ends down, to crimp into a fortune cookie shape (see above tutorial video if needed).

- Place the cookie in a muffin tin to let it cool and hold its shape.

- Repeat with the remaining batter and enjoy!

Romantic Inspiration

Mark Twain, one of America's greatest authors, and his wife, Olivia "Livy" Langdon, shared a love story as remarkable as his famous wit. They met in 1867, introduced by Olivia's brother, and from the start, Twain was captivated by Livy's grace, intellect, and kindness. Olivia came from a refined, wealthy family. At the same time, Twain had a rough-and-tumble life full of travel and adventure, having worked as a riverboat pilot and traveled across the American West. Their differences seemed insurmountable at first, but they soon discovered a deep mutual admiration that transcended social boundaries.

Twain courted Livy persistently, writing her numerous love letters filled with humor, passion, and sincerity. Their relationship blossomed, and after two years of courtship, they married in 1870. Livy became Twain's emotional anchor, his most devoted supporter, and a guiding influence on his work. Through years of financial troubles, personal loss, and triumphs, Twain's love and admiration for Livy remained steadfast, and he often expressed this devotion through beautiful, heartfelt letters. Their correspondence is filled with tender words and a profound sense of companionship, revealing a side of the famous author who was vulnerable, romantic, and grateful for the love of his life.

Mark Twain to Olivia Langdon Clemens, 1869:

"Livy darling, I have already mailed you a letter today, but I am obliged to write again, because just a few moments ago I sat by the window and looked up at the moon, and I could see your face reflected there; and in the whole universe there was nothing but you. I could have stretched out my arms and drawn you to my breast and said: 'Dear heart, I am yours forever, and if I had the universe to give, it should be yours and yours only.'"

Mark Twain to Olivia Langdon Clemens, 1870:

"Out of the depths of my happy heart wells a great tide of love and prayer for this priceless treasure that is confided to my life-long keeping. You cannot see its intangible waves as they flow towards you, darling, but in these lines, you will hear, as it were, the distant beating of the surf. What a garden you have made of this wilderness that was my life. What an enchanted world you have revealed to me. Your love has transfigured me."

Sexy Playlist Game

What You'll Need

- A music streaming account with playlist functionality.
- A three-minute timer.
- Pen and paper for keeping score (optional).

Directions

If you don't already have a sexy playlist, it's time to make one! This activity is the perfect excuse to update your list of go-to songs that set the right vibe. Start by sitting down together and adding songs that bring out a fun, flirtatious side, or create a mellow, intimate mood. Once you've built your playlist, let the games begin!

Take turns describing a song on the list without mentioning any words from the song title, album, or artist name. Your goal is to get your partner to guess the song based on your description. Share memories associated with the song, describe how it makes you feel, or even hint at the lyrics—just don't make it too easy! You might find yourself laughing as you stretch your creativity to the max.

To make it more interesting, set a timer for each round. If you'd like, keep score and see who has the sharpest memory or the best guessing skills. But remember, the real aim is to create a fun, open space for intimate conversation, so let the laughs and lighthearted vibes take the lead.

Spice it Up

Turn this into a sexy charades game! Try acting out the songs as if you're on a dance floor, using movements, expressions, and gestures. The more dramatic, the better! You'll likely discover a few new things about each other's sense of rhythm—and humor.

Conversation Starters

- *If our relationship had a theme song, what would it be? Why?*
- *What song would you choose for us in five years?*
- *What's a song that makes you think of me every time you hear it?*
- *What genre of music would you never want on our "sexy playlist"? Why?*

Romantic Projections

What You'll Need

- A projector (you can find affordable options online)
- A blank wall, sheet, or screen
- Cozy blankets, pillows, and cushions
- Your favorite movie snacks

Directions

With a cozy outdoor or indoor movie date, you can turn an ordinary movie night into a magical cinematic experience. Start by choosing where to set up your "theater." If you have a backyard, hang a sheet on a wall or between trees, creating an outdoor screen surrounded by stars and fresh air.

To stay warm, lay down blankets, pile on cushions, and bring out your favorite throws. If indoor comfort sounds better, transform your living room into a snug nest by building a pillow fort or creating a "movie den" on the floor with all the softest blankets you can find.

Prepare your movie menu together! Whoever picks the movie makes the snacks, so get creative. Whether it's buttered popcorn, classic candy, or homemade nachos, a little effort in the kitchen will add a personal touch to the night. Once everything's ready, turn on the lights, turn on the projector, and snuggle up with your partner.

To keep things romantic, pick a classic love story you both enjoy or one with a dreamy, star-crossed romance. Watching an iconic on-screen couple fall in love can bring you closer as you both get swept up in the story. If you're up for it, let each of you take a turn picking the movie for double the fun.

Spice it Up

Skip the rom-coms and pick a more adventurous, mysterious, or steamy movie instead. Watching something a little out of your comfort zone can add excitement to the night and give you both an excuse to snuggle closer during the more intense scenes.

Conversation Starters

Use these to spark playful discussions and deepen your connection:

- *"What's your all-time favorite movie couple?"*
- *"If we were characters in a romantic movie, who would we be, and why?"*
- *"What's your favorite movie quote about love?"*
- *"If you could write the ending to our love story, how would it go?"*

Channel Your Inner Movie Character

Draw inspiration from beloved movie lines like Mr. Darcy's heartfelt confession to Elizabeth: "You have bewitched me, body and soul..." Pretend to be your favorite characters for fun—maybe try reenacting a scene or two with your own twist. You could even make a little game out of it, quoting lines from famous love stories and seeing if your partner knows the movie.

Make It Last

End the night with a stroll under the stars if you're outside or a slow dance in the glow of the projector. With soft music playing in the background, let the romance linger long after the movie ends.

The Granny Project

Once upon a time, there were two grannies who were best friends. They were such good friends; they wanted their grandchildren to end up together. One of the grannies owned a beach house that she rented to the public, so she asked her granddaughter, Kelly, to help her clean it. The other granny came to help, and she brought her grandson, Jason.

Kelly and Jason were both assigned the task of fixing a fence outside. Kelly had no idea how to fix a fence, which of course, was no shock to anyone. So, she just talked to Jason while he was hard at work. She had come ready to clean, so her hair was a mess, and her clothes were stained and full of holes. She didn't feel confident or look her best, but she really liked Jason.

Kelly didn't know it at sixteen, but Jason was the love of her life. They went to the same high school and then the same college. They got married. Had kids. And they built an incredible life together- all thanks to some meddling grannies.

Once Upon a Time

What You'll Need

- Eye contact, a cozy and comfortable place to share some intentional time together, and an open heart.

Directions

Set the Scene: Find a comfortable spot that feels inviting, whether it's curled up on the couch with a blanket or out on a quiet evening walk. This activity is all about diving into your love story, piece by piece.

Choose a Story to Share: Think back to an important or memorable moment in your relationship—whether it's the first time you met, a funny misunderstanding, a nerve-wracking first date, or a shared adventure that brought you closer. Choose a moment that brings back fond memories or maybe even one that feels like it happened yesterday.

Tell Your Side of the Story: Now, tell your partner what it was like from *your* point of view. Yes, they were there, but they weren't inside your head! They haven't heard what you were thinking, how you were feeling, or the little details you noticed that day. Paint a vivid picture for them. Describe everything from how they looked and what they said to the emotions you experienced. Add humor, love, and even a little suspense to make the story fun and meaningful.

Example

"The most beautiful person in the world walked into the room, and for a moment, my heart stopped beating. I remember thinking,

'Don't make a fool of yourself!' And when you smiled at me, I could barely remember my own name."

Focus on Feelings Over Facts: This isn't about recounting the details accurately; it's about sharing how you *felt*. Talk about the butterflies, the excitement, the nervousness, or the humor you remember. Share things like, "I was so nervous that my hands wouldn't stop shaking," or "I remember laughing so hard because you made me feel like I could just be myself."

Spice It Up

Tell the Story of Your First Intimate Moment: This doesn't mean going overboard with details but bringing a little romance or humor to those vulnerable and close moments you shared. Talk about the excitement, the laughter, and the special bond it created.

Narrate Your Present Actions in a Playful Way: Try narrating what's happening between you right now as if it were a love story. Pretend to be the voiceover in a romantic movie: "As they shared this quiet moment together, wrapped in cozy blankets, he looked into her eyes and knew he was exactly where he was meant to be." It's playful, a bit silly, and fun, and can help you both see the beauty in your everyday interactions.

Love Story Idea: A Tale of Meddling Grannies

Once upon a time, there were two best friends—both grandmothers—who had a grand plan. They wanted their grandchildren, Kelly and Jason, to end up together. One granny owned a little beach house she rented out, and she asked her granddaughter, Kelly, to help her clean it for the summer. The other granny joined, bringing her grandson, Jason, along to help with some fix-ups.

Kelly and Jason were both assigned the task of fixing a rickety old fence outside. Kelly, who knew absolutely nothing about fixing fences, did her best to "help" Jason by simply chatting with him while he worked. She was dressed in her messiest clothes, with her hair up in a loose, careless bun, feeling far from her most confident self. But somehow, Jason didn't seem to mind.

They were just sixteen, both too young to know that they were destined to be each other's loves. Over time, they went to the same high school, then the same college, and eventually got married. Now, many years and memories later, they look back and realize that a small moment at that beach house led to a lifetime of love— all thanks to two meddling grannies who knew just what they were doing.

Conversation Starters

To keep the fun going, here are some lighthearted prompts to explore together:

- *If our love story was made into a movie, who would play me?*
- *Who would play you?*
- *What song would play during our first meeting?*
- *What's the funniest thing you remember about our early dates?*
- *If you could relive one moment from our relationship, what would it be?*
- *What do you think made us such a great match from the beginning?*

Reflection on the Power of Your Love Story

There's something uniquely special about hearing a story from your partner's perspective, especially when it's one you both shared. Seeing yourself through their eyes can be a powerful reminder of why you fell in love in the first place. By reliving these memories, you're reconnecting and deepening your relationship in a way that few things can.

Afterward, take a moment to savor the shared laughter, the sweet nostalgia, and even the happy tears. These stories of your love are like precious keepsakes, reminders of how far you've come and all the beautiful memories yet to come.

Most likely to...

What You'll Need

- Four small objects to represent each of you, two for each person:
- Two dimes and two pennies
- Two red poker chips and two green poker chips
- Two buttons and two thimbles
- Two paperclips and two pen caps

Setting the Scene

Dim the lights, put on some music that fits your vibe—whether it's relaxing or playful—and sit across from each other, ready for a night of laughter and unexpected revelations! Pour your favorite drinks or prepare some snacks to add to the relaxed, fun vibe. Grab a cozy blanket if it's chilly or play your favorite playlist in the background. This game is all about seeing each other from a new, sometimes hilariously absurd perspective, so dive in with an open mind.

Directions

Choose Your Objects: Start by picking two small objects to represent each person. Each person will have two—one for themselves and one for their partner. These objects are essential because they allow you to vote secretly for who's "most likely" for each scenario.

Sit Opposite Each Other: Take a comfortable seat across from each other. The closer, the better, as it'll be easier to read each other's expressions and make this fun and intimate.

Choose Your First "Most Likely To...": One of you starts by saying, "Most likely to..." and fills in the blank with something wild, unexpected, or funny. You can be as imaginative as you like, or even a little mischievous—think of something that might make you both laugh or spark a playful debate!

Cast Your Vote: Both of you secretly palm the object representing either yourself or your partner, depending on who you think best fits the prompt. When you're ready, count to three and reveal your votes simultaneously.

Laugh, Debate, and Reflect: Most likely, your choices won't always match! This is where the fun starts—laugh together, share stories, and enjoy the little debates about why one of you is "definitely" the one more likely to fall down the stairs, cry in a movie, or say something awkward in front of strangers. The beauty of this game is in the stories you uncover about each other.

Spice It Up

Want to take it to the next level? Here's a spicy twist: turn up the heat by adding some cheeky, flirtatious prompts. Stick with the same concept, but think up some playful scenarios like:

- *"Most likely to suggest a spontaneous trip?"*
- *"Most likely to buy something just for fun?"*
- *"Most likely to buy a sexy outfit?"*

This variation adds a bit of intimacy and lets you explore each other's daring sides. Feel free to come up with your own ideas for fun, spicy prompts.

Conversation Starters

To keep the laughs and conversation going, throw in these prompts:

- *"When did you last do something totally unexpected?"*

- *"What's one thing you think would surprise most people about you?"*
- *"What's the weirdest thing you've ever bought on a whim?"*

These open more fun stories and help you get to know each other in unexpected ways.

Prompts List (Suggestions & Ideas)

Feel free to create your own, but here are some fun "Most Likely To" ideas to get you started:

- *Get a face tattoo?*
- *Accidentally say something embarrassing in public?*
- *Walk out of a movie because it was so bad?*
- *Eat the last cookie without asking?*
- *Get lost in the grocery store?*
- *Go viral on social media?*
- *Win a dance-off at a party?*
- *Laugh so hard that they snort?*
- *Forget their phone at home?*
- *Be mistaken for a celebrity?*

Group Variation

This game can be easily adapted for a night in with friends. With a bigger group, it only gets more entertaining, as you'll get to see how everyone perceives each other! Mix up the prompts with some about group dynamics like "Most likely to...":

- *Be the first to make a fool of themselves at karaoke?*
- *Organize the next road trip?*
- *Show up the latest to a party?*

Adding this group version brings everyone closer and creates shared memories that'll spark laughter for ages!

Photo Shoot

What You'll Need

- A camera or smartphone with a good camera.
- Outfits for a range of looks (think: casual, formal, silly, and surprise!)
- Scrapbooking supplies: stickers, washi tape, markers, and embellishments to personalize your pages.

Directions

Start by picking out outfits for each other and get ready for your photoshoot! Have fun with each choice—mix in your favorite looks, surprising themes, or even unexpected styles that you wouldn't normally choose. You could even make it a game: each of you gets five minutes to "style" the other person for a photo-worthy outfit.

Once dressed up, one of you will start as the model while the other takes on the role of photographer. Experiment with different poses, settings, and expressions. If you're up for a little adventure, try staging shots in different rooms, around the house, or at a scenic outdoor spot. Switch roles halfway through, and don't forget to capture some classic couples' shots with a timer. The goofier, the better—be playful, make faces, and catch candid moments.

When your photos are ready, print them out (or pick your favorites to print later), and get out your scrapbooking supplies. Together, create a scrapbook of your photo shoot, adding captions, doodles, and funny inside jokes. Capture the memories and laughs that went into each shot!

Spice it up

If you're both feeling adventurous, try a boudoir-inspired shoot. Lingerie or a bare-it-all theme can add an intimate twist. Just remember to handle these photos with care if you decide to print them—be aware of any potential "audience" at the print shop!

For an added playful twist, try setting themes for each "round" of photos. Perhaps a celebrity look-alike contest, re-creating scenes from movies, or even "time travel" outfits from different decades. It's all about letting go, getting creative, and having fun together!

Creating Memories

Scrapbooking these photos is your opportunity to build something together that reflects your unique relationship. Will your scrapbook turn out wacky, sweet, steamy, or all of the above? There's no right or wrong—it's about enjoying the process of making memories together and capturing them in a way that feels true to you both.

Conversation Starters

- *What's your all-time favorite outfit of mine?*
- *What kind of photoshoots should we try next—outdoor, travel, or maybe underwater?*
- *If we could go anywhere in the world for a photo shoot, where would you pick?*

Word for Word

What You'll Need

- A pen and paper
- OR a laptop/notebook to type it out
- A cozy spot to sit together

Directions

Start with one person saying a word—any word. Then, the other person adds a word. Keep going back and forth, word by word, building up a story that's uniquely yours. One of you can be the "scribe" to write or type out each word as it's spoken and watch as your wild, random story unfolds. Your goal? To keep the story coherent (at least somewhat), while having as much fun as possible.

At the end, you'll have a quirky story that reflects both of your styles and personalities. Make it a tradition by keeping each story in a special notebook or binder, creating a fun archive you can revisit to relive these creative memories.

Spice It Up

Want to add a bit of romance? Write a sexy story with yourselves as the main characters. Think of this as a chance to step into a fantasy world together, where you can be spies on a mission, explorers in a far-off jungle, or whatever you dream up!

Why It Works

This activity takes teamwork and creativity, and no matter where the story goes, you're bound to share a few laughs. Laughter is an amazing way to bond, and seeing where your story twists and turns will show you know sides of each other's personalities. Your final story may not make perfect sense, but that's part of the fun! It's all about sharing and connecting in a relaxed, creative way.

Conversation Starters

After your story, spark deeper conversation with these questions:

- *If you could rewrite part of our real-life love story, would you? If so, which part?*
- *What's something you'd never want to change about our relationship?*
- *What's the craziest adventure you'd want us to go on together in real life?*

Romantic Inspiration

Modern Day Romantics

Though sometimes communicated in different ways—through social media posts, memoirs, or intimate letters—these modern love stories show that romance, connection, and passion can thrive across generations. They inspire people today to express their love in ways that transcend time, whether through handwritten letters or thoughtful digital messages.

Johnny Cash and June Carter Cash

- *One of the most iconic love stories of modern times, Johnny Cash and June Carter Cash's relationship was filled with devotion and passion. Cash famously wrote beautiful letters to June, even after years of marriage. One of his most famous letters, written on June's 65th birthday, reads:*

- *"We get old and get used to each other. We think alike. We read each other's minds. We know what the other wants without asking. Sometimes, we irritate each other a little bit. Maybe sometimes take each other for granted. But once in a while, like today, I meditate on it and realize how lucky I am to share my life with the greatest woman I ever met."*

- *Their love was one of music, mutual admiration, and deep friendship, with their story made famous in movies like Walk the Line.*

Barack and Michelle Obama

- *The former U.S. president and first lady have a modern love story that has captured the hearts of many. While they may not have love letters as famously published as those from historical figures, Barack and Michelle's story is one of partnership,* admiration, and mutual respect. In Barack Obama's memoir *A Promised Land*, he reflects on how Michelle has been his constant support. On multiple occasions, he has publicly expressed his deep love for her, often speaking about her in heartfelt terms, like when he said:

- *"Like everyone else, Michelle has a way of grounding me, reminding me of what's important, keeping me humble, reminding me of the responsibility I have not just as a husband and father, but as a leader."*

Finger Painting

What You'll Need

- Body-safe paint (or even better, edible body paint!)

Directions

Ready to let your creativity run wild—and right onto each other? Grab some body paint, spread it on a plate or palette, and let the fun begin! Start painting every inch of your partner's body. Each brushstroke can be a playful shape, a swirl, or maybe even a heart on their shoulder or a flower on their cheek. When you're done, swap places and see who can make the most playful, vibrant "canvas."

You can take it slow, adding small, intricate designs, or go big and colorful, creating "masterpieces" that only you both can appreciate. Remember, it's not about perfection—it's about exploring touch and closeness and seeing what fun surprises come up as you paint!

Spice it Up

If you're feeling bold, switch out the body paint for edible options like chocolate or flavored body paint. This way, you can mix a little art with a little taste—each stroke has the potential to turn into a playful bite or kiss.

Conversation Starters

- *What's the most ridiculous thing you've ever done for love?*
- *Was it worth it? Would you do it again?*

- *If you had to describe our love with a color or shape, what would it be?*
- *Maybe a heart, an infinity symbol, or something totally unique to you both!*
- *What's one thing about us that you think only we could ever understand?*
- *Share those quirks or habits that only make sense in your relationship.*
- *If we could design one thing to hang in our home from this painting session, what would it be?*
- *It might inspire some silly art you can laugh at for years to come!*

Room for Two

What You'll Need

- A hotel reservation
- Your favorite dress-up clothes
- A few creative ideas (and maybe a secret backstory!)

Directions

Step into the world of adventure by booking a night at a nearby hotel and transforming the evening into an unforgettable escape from reality. Dress to impress and pick a spot to "meet" your partner – a local bar or a cozy restaurant works perfectly. But tonight, you're strangers with a twist! Play the role of two intriguing characters who just happened to cross paths.

Take things slow and embrace your new identities. Who are you tonight? A globe-trotting mystery novelist? A French art dealer on a secret mission? Go as big (or as quirky) as you'd like! Enjoy getting to "know" each other again through fresh eyes, share exaggerated stories, and dive into the thrill of being somewhere and someone completely different.

When the night winds down, don't break character – let the suspense build as you slip back to the hotel together, still in the mystery of your alternate personas.

Spice it Up

Amp up the night with a few extras:

- **New Lingerie or Outfits:** Something your character would wear – think glamorous, bold, or even a little out of your comfort zone.
- **Accessories and Props:** Try wigs, glasses, hats, or even temporary tattoos to really embody your alter-ego.
- **Fake Names & Accents:** Pick a name you've always loved, add a convincing accent, and play it up. Your new alias might just reveal a daring side you didn't know you had.

Conversation Starters

Get to know each other as your "new selves" with these fun questions:

- *"If you could be anyone in the world for a day, who would you choose to be? Why?"*
- *"What's one adventure you'd love to take but haven't yet?"*
- *"If you could only keep one memory from your past, what would it be?"*
- *"What's the most surprising thing someone would never guess about you?"*

This isn't just about pretending – it's about exploring and rediscovering each other in a way that brings fresh excitement and a spark of adventure.

Dream Vacation

What You'll Need

- A budgeting app or notebook
- Possibly a passport
- A shared folder or Pinterest board for your travel inspiration

Directions

Set aside an evening, pour your favorite drinks, and start your journey together by imagining the ultimate dream vacation. Start with the basics: would it be a cozy winter wonderland or a tropical beach escape? Is there a particular city, country, or experience you've both been dreaming about?

Together, do some online exploring! Look up places to stay, things to do, and even foods to try. Dive into the details—what local foods are a must? What sights or activities make the destination unique? Add these ideas to your shared folder or board to keep track of your discoveries. Once you've got the dream outlined, estimate the costs: flights, accommodations, food, adventures, and any necessary extras like childcare or pet care.

Next, plan to save for your getaway. Set aside a set amount each month toward the trip—whether it's $5 or $50, consistency is key. Create a cute countdown tracker you both can update together as you get closer to reaching your goal. It doesn't matter if it takes years to save up; just having this shared goal is a fantastic bonding experience that will give you something exciting to look forward to.

Spice It Up

Make date nights themed around your future destination! For example, if it's Italy, cook pasta together and plan a movie night with a travel documentary about Italy. As a mini splurge, set aside a little extra for a luxury treat on your trip, like a couples' massage or a private dinner with a view. This will give your planning an added touch of romance and make saving feel even more fun.

Conversation Starters

- *If you could visit one place in the world right now, where would it be, and why?*
- *What's one travel adventure you'd love to try together—hiking, snorkeling, a road trip?*
- *What kind of experiences would make a trip truly memorable for you?*

Remember

Dreaming together is just as powerful as the trip itself. Let yourselves imagine the possibilities without focusing on timelines or barriers.

Romantic Inspiration

The romantic story of *James Joyce and Nora Barnacle* is one of passion, devotion, and literary inspiration. Their relationship began in 1904 when Joyce, a struggling writer in Dublin, encountered Nora, a hotel chambermaid from Galway. On June 10, 1904, they went on their first date, and Nora later said that it was the day they first shared an intimate moment, an event that Joyce would later immortalize in his work.

Joyce was immediately captivated by Nora's earthy personality and independence. She was uneducated but intelligent and had a straightforwardness that Joyce found refreshing compared to the pretentiousness of Dublin society. He referred to her as his "Simple Wildflower," and despite the differences in their backgrounds, they quickly developed a powerful connection.

Shortly after meeting, Joyce left Dublin to pursue his writing career in continental Europe, and Nora, remarkably, agreed to join him. They eloped to Zurich, then moved to Trieste, Italy, where Joyce began writing some of his most famous works. Throughout their life together, which included periods of financial instability and the challenges of raising two children, Nora remained Joyce's muse and emotional anchor.

Nora inspired some of Joyce's iconic characters, notably Molly Bloom in *Ulysses*. Their passionate, often volatile relationship was marked by Joyce's deep reliance on her for emotional and creative support. Despite his many literary accomplishments, Joyce frequently turned to Nora for validation and inspiration, writing her a series of love letters that ranged from tenderly romantic to erotically explicit.

Through all the challenges—Joyce's complex personality, poor health, financial struggles, and a long separation during World War I—Nora stood by him. They finally married in 1931, after 27 years together, though they always referred to each other as husband and wife. Their love story remains one of the most passionate and tumultuous in literary history, showing how love can fuel great art!

James Joyce to Nora Barnacle, December 2, 1909:

"You are my only love. You have me completely in your power. I know and feel that if I am to write anything fine and noble in the future I shall do so only by listening at the doors of your heart. I would like to lie down there beside you, darling, and die, one hand resting on your quiet breast and the other on your warm womb, hearing your soft words, which I am sure would comfort me at the last. You are my life, my everything. From the first moment I heard your voice I felt your soul enter into mine."

For some examples of his more erotic confessions of love: **"James Joyce: The Letters, Volumes I, II, and III" (1966)**: *These volumes, also edited by Richard Ellmann, offer a more comprehensive collection of Joyce's letters, including those of a more risqué nature. Additionally, searching specifically for "James Joyce's erotic letters to Nora Barnacle" might lead you to articles or blog posts that delve into the content of these famous letters*

Chef Master

What You'll Need

- Friends to judge
- A place to cook (kitchen or grill area)
- A list of fun, versatile ingredients (lemons, chocolate, fish, tomatoes, etc.)
- Cooking essentials (pots, pans, and plating items)

Directions

Choose the Ingredient of the Night: Start by selecting a "mystery" ingredient you'll both use in each course. You could go classic with chocolate or tomatoes or make it extra challenging with something like chili peppers or avocados.

Divide and Conquer: Each of you will create three courses using the secret ingredient in every dish: an appetizer, a main course, and a dessert. Get as creative as you can! Maybe it's chocolate-dipped bacon for an appetizer or spicy avocado brownies for dessert. Don't reveal your ideas to each other – the element of surprise is part of the fun!

Set the Scene for Judging: Invite a few friends to join you as judges, turning your kitchen into an at-home restaurant. To make things interesting, try serving on identical plates without tipping off which dish is whose! Watch their faces and see if they can guess who made what.

Declare the Chef Master: After tasting each dish, your friends will vote on the Chef Master. The winner gets bragging rights... until the next cook-off!

Spice it Up

- **A Date for Two:** Instead of inviting friends, make it a special dinner for just the two of you. Dress up your table with a fancy tablecloth, flowers, and candlelight for a little romance. Take turns serving each course, and add a twist with blindfolded tastings to heighten the mystery!

- **International Theme Night:** Pick a country as your culinary inspiration, and each course must include both the special ingredient and a traditional element from that cuisine! You'll bond over learning new recipes and techniques, making it an exciting (and sometimes funny) culinary adventure.

Conversation Starters

- *What unique ingredient would you say represents "us" as a couple?*

- *If we could go to any country to explore its cuisine together, where would we go?*

- *What's your funniest or strangest food memory?*

Little Things

What You'll Need

- Creativity and Thoughtfulness
- Writing materials (stationery, envelopes, stamps)
- A camera or smartphone for taking pictures
- Flowers or small gifts (optional)
- A list of shared memories (to inspire your notes)

Directions

This activity is all about the little ways you can express your love for your partner. It focuses on creativity and personal touches, with the goal of making them feel cherished through thoughtful gestures that brighten their day.

Write a Love Letter: Channel your inner romantic by penning a heartfelt letter. Share what you love about them, recall fond memories, or express your hopes for the future. For an extra touch, mail it to them or leave it in a surprising spot, like their car or briefcase, to discover later.

Send a Card: Buy or make a card that resonates with your relationship. You could create a handmade card featuring an inside joke, a memorable photo, or a theme that represents a special moment you've shared. Make sure to write a personal message inside—something sweet, funny, or meaningful that reminds them of your bond.

Surprise Flowers: Arrange for flowers to be delivered to your home or workplace. Choose blooms that have significance, like their favorite flower or ones that remind you of a special occasion. When they receive them, share a note that explains why you chose those specific flowers to create a deeper connection.

Random Gifts: Get them a small, thoughtful present "just because." It could be a favorite snack, a book you've discussed, or something related to their hobby. Present it in a unique way—wrap it in an unusual package or hide it in an unexpected place for them to find.

Change Their Phone Wallpaper: Take a fresh photo of yourself (perhaps in a cute or silly pose) and change their phone wallpaper to this image. This way, they'll think of you every time they check their phone!

Create a Shared Memory Jar: Write down little memories or moments you cherish together on separate slips of paper. Fill a jar with these notes, and encourage your loved one to take one out whenever they need a reminder of your love.

Creative Messages: Leave sticky notes around the house with sweet messages, jokes, or reminders of inside jokes. They could be hidden in places like the bathroom mirror, inside a shoe, or on the fridge.

Spice it Up

To add a fun twist to your expressions of love, consider using a privacy screen for their phone. Change their wallpaper to a cheeky or sexy photo of yourself wearing lingerie or something playful that will spark their interest. This will not only surprise them but will also serve as a fun anticipation for your evening together!

Additional Thoughts

When it comes to saying, "I love you," the little things truly mean the most. Use some of these ideas or come up with your own ways to show your partner how you feel. Make sure to personalize each gesture to reflect your unique relationship. However you say it, say it sincerely, and say it often.

Conversation Starters

- *What makes you feel loved?*
- *Is there anything I used to do for you that you miss?*
- *Can you remember a time when a small gesture from me made your day?*
- *What's your favorite way to receive affection?*

Chore Swap

What You'll Need

- Nothing but a bit of patience, a touch of humor, and maybe a playful wink.

How to Play?

Find Your 'Not-So-Favorite' Tasks: Start by pinpointing those little household chores you each dread (or forget!) doing. Don't be shy; be honest about what you could use a hand with or what you might conveniently "forget" every now and then. Feel free to laugh about each other's "chore blind spots" while you're at it!

Switch It Up: For one whole week, take on the task your partner finds annoying or often overlooks. Let them take over one of yours in return. If you both hate the same chore (like scrubbing the bathtub or tackling that pile of mail), do it together! It's amazing how much faster a dreaded job can go when you're working side-by-side with someone you love.

Make It Personal: Add a twist to keep it fresh and fun! Decide on one small "extra" to do for each other. It could be leaving a note near the chore once it's done, adding a little surprise (like putting on a favorite song), or just adding a personal touch to the routine. Make it sweet, silly, or anything that feels like you!

Spice It Up

- **Give Directions:** For a fun twist, tell your partner exactly how you like things done—and let them do the same for you! It's a playful way to understand each other's preferences and perhaps find a new appreciation for the work you both put in.

- **Create a Reward:** When the week is up, treat each other to a small reward for a job well done—whether that's a movie night, a cozy dinner, or just a celebratory hug for surviving each other's pet peeves!

Conversation Starters

- *What's the one chore you'd love to never do again?*
- *Are there any chores that you secretly enjoy?*
- *What chore would you like to make into a team activity?*
- *How do you feel when I take care of one of your "least favorite" tasks?*

Love Story: Mia and David

Mia can never seem to remember to put her clothes in the dryer. She's great at starting a load, but for some reason, coming back to transfer them is just a step that tends to slip her mind. After one too many instances of souring clothes, her husband David took over the task. At first, he was frustrated; it seemed so simple! But Mia reminded him, "We all have our little things," and pointed out that he often forgets his own task: making tea.

David loves tea, but his routine is a bit hit-or-miss. He'll get the pot going, add the bags, and then... forget all about it. Eventually, Mia began to brew his tea for him when he wandered off. Over time, the two stopped feeling irritated over each other's missed steps. It became a game, almost an inside joke, as they covered each other's "blind spots" with a laugh and a sense of care.

Now, whenever Mia finds a pot of forgotten tea on the stove, she rolls her eyes and finishes it for him. They've created their own rhythm, a way of saying, "I've got you covered." It's a little thing, but together, they've turned it into something special—a unique, practical language of love.

Blackout

What You'll Need

A few candles to set the mood

Activities that don't require electricity, like books, puzzles, or a deck of cards

Directions

Turn off all lights and set aside any tech devices—no phones, TVs, or computers. It's time to escape the digital world together.

Light your candles to create a warm, intimate atmosphere.

Plan a few simple, tech-free activities: a cozy candlelit picnic, a board game, reading to each other, or a storytelling session. Most importantly, make eye contact, laugh, and enjoy each other's presence without distractions.

Spice It Up

For an extra twist, have one partner wear a blindfold or close their eyes while the other vividly describes your planned evening. The "listener" will practice being present and engaged, focusing on their partner's words and emotions, heightening your connection through focused attention.

A New Evening Ritual

Replace your typical screen time with an evening of true connection. Focus on quality conversation and eye contact to rediscover each other in a whole new way. By shifting away from screens, you may even find that your mind feels clearer and that you sleep better tonight.

Conversation Starters

- *Would you like to incorporate more tech-free time into our routine?*
- *What's one way we could be intentional about creating more unplugged moments?*

Let your imagination lead the way and savor this time together—no notifications, just the two of you.

Volunteer

What You'll Need

- Kindness, a sense of adventure, and a willingness to get your hands a little dirty.

Directions

Choose Together: Find a cause that lights you both up! Sit down with your partner and share what drives you. Is it animal rescue, environmental cleanup, or helping kids learn to read? Choose an organization or event together to volunteer with. It's a great way to discover new things about each other.

Reach Out: Contact the chosen organization and learn about volunteer opportunities. This could be a one-time event or an ongoing project, but either way, you'll have a memorable experience to share.

Jump In: Whether it's planting trees, cooking at a soup kitchen, or organizing donations, dive in with enthusiasm. You'll support a cause you both care about while building teamwork skills.

Spice It Up

When your volunteer day is over, plan a "thank you" moment for your partner. This could be as simple as a cozy night in or a surprise treat. Celebrate the connection you've deepened through giving back.

Blackout Together

Focus on each other and the cause—no distractions!

On the day of your volunteer project, agree to go "blackout"—turn off your phones and step away from screens. The digital detox will help you stay present, focus on each other, and fully connect with the impact you're making together.

Conversation Starters

- *What are you passionate about? If you could solve one problem in the world, what would it be?*
- *Who has made the biggest difference in your life? How have they inspired you?*
- *What's a childhood memory that makes you happy? How do you feel about doing something similar to help others?*

By sharing meaningful work, you'll not only give back but also create a powerful experience that strengthens your bond and opens conversations you may never have had.

Nailed It

What You'll Need

- Baking tools
- A hilariously complicated recipe (think 5-tier cakes, cartoon character cookies, or an artful pie!)
- A hefty dose of humor

Directions

This activity is inspired by the chaotic joy of the "Nailed It!" competition show. The aim is simple: pick a recipe that's leagues beyond your comfort zone. The more ambitious, the better!

Challenge: Try decorating cookies to look like each other or tackling a towering cake with no fear of the (inevitable) mess. You can make it a head-to-head competition in front of friends or join forces for a true baking "masterpiece."

Time yourself and get started! Remember, the messier, the funnier—and that's the goal. Laughing through this activity together will have you both feeling closer, maybe even with a sugary treat at the end!

Spice It Up

Make extra icing and get creative! Will icing pies catch on? They will be in your kitchen. You can even use that leftover frosting to sneak a playful smear on your baking buddy.

Embrace the Fail

When success isn't in the cards, the hilarity comes free! This is all about bonding over the chaos. Even if your dessert looks a little... abstract, you'll enjoy every second of creating it (and probably eating it, too!).

Conversation Starters

- *What's the last thing you tried but were totally bad at?*
- *If we learned a new skill together, what would you want to try?*
- *Would you ever consider signing us up for a couples' cooking class?*

"Success is always less funny than failure."

– Jon Ronson

Trash to Treasure

What You'll Need

- A trip to an antique store or flea market
- Fifty dollars (split equally between you!)
- Access to tools (or just work with what you've got)
- Crafting supplies (optional, for extra flair)

Directions

Set the Scene: Each of you has $25 to find an item with hidden potential. Whether it's a dusty lamp, a quirky frame, or a vintage knick-knack, the goal is to see past the "junk" and find something you can repurpose or reimagine.

Get Crafty: Take your items home and use whatever tools and materials you have. Be resourceful! The fun is in the transformation. Don't worry if you aren't a DIY expert; this is about creativity, not perfection.

Show It Off: Post your finished pieces online to see if you can make a profit! This not only makes the experience more exciting, but it can also fund your next date night.

Declare the Winner: Whoever makes the most profit from selling their creation wins! But remember, you both win if you're having fun together.

Spice it Up!

For an extra twist, use the profit toward a fun experience you both enjoy—maybe a cozy dinner, a new adventure, or even supplies for your next project. Or, if you both love the pieces too much to sell, keep them in a special place in your home as a memory of your shared creativity.

Conversation Starters

Turn on some music, grab your tools, and keep the laughs going with these conversation starters while you work:

- *Do you prefer old things or new things? Why?*
- *What's the most valuable thing you've ever created?*
- *If you had to pick one item in our home to "upcycle," what would it be?*

With Trash to Treasure, it's not just about the finished product but about the laughter, problem-solving, and collaboration along the way. Plus, you get to see each other's quirky, creative side!

Trivia Night

What You'll Need

- Your favorite trivia spot or event
- A few friends for added fun (optional)
- Snacks or drinks to fuel your brainpower

Directions

Locate a local trivia event and dust off that random knowledge in the back of your mind. How many colors are in the rainbow? Who was the 22nd U.S. president? Who thought to first brew coffee? As you work through each question, remember tonight's not about genius—it's about laughs, teamwork, and maybe even learning a little more about your partner. Plus, depending on the trivia night, you could walk away with some extra cash or prizes!

Spice It Up

For a more personal twist, bring the trivia home! Stand across the room from each other and answer questions related to each other's quirks, favorites, and "us" moments. Each correct answer means a step closer, but a wrong answer? Step back! The first one to reach their partner wins a special prize—it is up to you to decide.

Conversation Starters

Keep the conversation going with these fun questions.

- *Do you consider yourself an expert on anything?*
- *What's one totally useless fact you've memorized?*

- *What trivia would you use to stump me?*

"You're the only thing I know like the back of my hand."

—*Taylor Swift,* Breathe

Add this trivia twist to your date nights, and before long, you'll be pros not just at answering questions—but at learning more about each other in ways you might not expect!

Romantic Inspiration

John and Abigail Adams

Sometimes referred to as the original Power Couple, the couple exchanged over 1,100 letters during their courtship and marriage (often addressing her as 'my dearest partner'), which provided a unique window into their lives and the founding of the United States.

John and Abigail Adams are not contemporary figures, although their prolific exchange of love letters has inspired couples in modern times. Famous romantic couples like Paul Newman and Joanne Woodward or Jimmy and Rosalind Carter have cited the importance of letters and communication in keeping their relationship strong. Both Newman and Carter often wrote letters and notes to their wives, even after many years of marriage, emphasizing how this practice can be kept alive in modern times.

John Adams affectionately called Abigail "Miss Adorable" and wrote, "I hereby order you to give me as many kisses and as many hours of your company as I shall please to demand and charge them to my account.

Stargazing

What You'll Need

- A fluffy blanket
- A clear, dark night
- A telescope (optional, for the astronomy buffs)
- Wine or hot chocolate (because why not?)

Directions

Find Your Spot: Head out to a place with minimal light pollution—maybe a scenic overlook or an open field. If you're lucky enough to live near mountains or beaches, those can be perfect, too.

Set the Scene: Spread out your blanket and get cozy. Pour a glass of wine (or hot chocolate), wrap up in the blanket together, and settle in for a night of stargazing and shared moments.

Make it Yours: Name a star after your partner. Point it out and make a wish together; the sappiness is half the fun!

Spice it Up

- **Get Creative with Constellations:** Make up your own constellations and give them funny names. Instead of hunting for the Big Dipper, maybe you'll find the "Eternal Sock" or "Mystic Pancake."
- **A Starry Promise:** Take turns sharing a little dream or promise for the future under the stars.

Conversation Starters

Here's where the fun really begins. Get to know each other better with these questions:

- *"Did you ever dream of being an astronaut when you were a kid? What changed?"*
- *"What was the coolest job you imagined having as a child? If you could still do it, would you?"*
- *"Is there a star or planet that feels like it fits your personality?"*

Bonus Challenge

Trivia Night, Star Edition!

If you're looking for a fun challenge, turn stargazing into a trivia game! Mix in random trivia questions for each other, like famous constellations or Hollywood stars. This can lead to a lot of laughter, especially when the "facts" get creative!

The Pieces Just Fit

What You'll Need
- A fun or memorable puzzle of your choice
- Puzzle storage mat (optional)
- Puzzle glue (optional)

Directions

Next time you're out, grab a puzzle or order one online. For a twist, consider using a custom print shop to turn a cherished photo of you two into a jigsaw puzzle. This makes the experience even more meaningful, as each piece brings you closer to the final image of a shared memory.

Spend an evening—or maybe a week, depending on the puzzle size—together, pouring over the pieces and watching the picture take shape. When it's complete, you can glue it together and frame it as a lasting memento of your teamwork and time together.

Spice it up: Choose a fun or quirky puzzle! It could be an image that makes you laugh or a puzzle you wouldn't necessarily want hanging in your living room. That way, the activity is both entertaining and lighthearted, adding an unexpected element to your evening.

Take a Break from the Screen!

Turn off the TV, roll up your sleeves, and dive into a bit of teamwork. Puzzles are a great way to get talking, strategizing, and just enjoying each other's company. Consider taking turns picking out puzzles or creating a surprise custom one that reveals a special memory or inside joke between you.

Conversation Starters

Here are a few questions to make the experience even more interesting:

- *What's something puzzling about me?*
- *What are some ways we could connect more?*

Have fun and make this puzzle night a unique way to connect, laugh, and maybe even learn something new about each other.

Bad Movie Night

What You'll Need
- A hilariously bad movie
- Your favorite snacks and drinks

Directions

If you're not sure where to find a "bad" movie, a quick search for cult classics or "worst-rated films" will give you a goldmine of options. The key is finding a movie that's so outrageous or over-the-top that it turns unintentional comedy into shared laughs. Grab your popcorn, curl up on the couch, and get ready to bond over the absurdity.

Spice It Up

If the movie becomes unbearable (not all bad movies are charmingly bad), switch things up! You can try guessing the plot twists, reenacting ridiculous scenes, or even making a game of creating alternative endings. Remember, the goal isn't to watch the movie—it's to connect, laugh, and enjoy each other's company.

Take It to the Next Level
- *Rating System:* Rate each scene on a scale from 1-10, where 1 is hilariously terrible and 10 is accidentally brilliant.
- *Mystery Commentary:* Channel your inner "Mystery Science Theater" host and provide commentary during the movie. Create backstories for characters, mock plot holes, or invent what the characters are really thinking.

Conversation Starters for Extra Fun

- What are your top three favorite movies, and what makes them so great?
- Now, reveal three guilty pleasure movies you would never admit to anyone else.

Blind Taste Test

What You'll Need

- A variety of bite-sized foods (cheeses, wines, smoked meats, fruits, chocolates, or candies)
- A blindfold (A scarf or sleep mask works well!)

Directions

Lay out an assortment of foods that you and your partner will taste. The more flavors and textures, the better!

Take turns blindfolding each other. Once blindfolded, one partner feeds the other a small piece of food and asks them to guess what it is. Make sure to mix up the order to keep things challenging.

Keep score of correct guesses, if you like.

After both of you have had a turn, tally the points to see who has the sharper taste buds!

Spice It Up

When you're both feeling comfortable, try removing an item of clothing with each round, or keep the blindfold on after the game to heighten other senses and enjoy a bit more closeness.

Why It's Fun

Testing your taste buds is a playful way to connect, learn something new about each other, and share a few laughs. The blindfold adds an element of trust and mystery, encouraging vulnerability and presence in the moment.

Conversation Starters for Closer Connection

After your taste test, dive into a few fun questions to keep the mood light and the conversation flowing!

- *If you could only eat three foods for the rest of your life, what would they be?*
- *What's one food you used to hate but now love?*
- *If you could only drink one thing (besides water), what would it be?*
- *Is there a specific taste that reminds you of a favorite memory?*

Adding a mix of fun conversation starters and playful rules to the game gives couples an easy way to deepen their bond. This activity isn't just about enjoying food; it's about experiencing shared laughter, building trust, and creating memories together. Enjoy!

Personal Stylist

What You'll Need

- A clothing budget (set a fun limit)
- A local mall or boutique store
- A sense of adventure and a willingness to step outside your comfort zone!

Directions

Hit the Mall: Make a date out of this adventure! Head to your local mall or a quirky boutique. The goal? Find an outfit for your partner that pushes their style boundaries—something they wouldn't typically wear.

Turn the Tables: Take turns being the stylist. Each partner will have a designated time (15-20 minutes) to scour the store for the perfect ensemble. Don't hold back! This is your chance to unleash your creativity and show your partner how you envision their fabulous self.

Style Selection: When it's your turn, remember the only rule:

Stay within budget! You can pick everything from clothing to shoes and accessories. The catch? Your partner can't influence your choices—this is all about trusting your judgment.

Fashion Show Dinner: Once you've made your selections, head out for dinner or drinks together in your chosen outfits! This adds an extra layer of excitement as you both strut your stuff in unexpected attire. Capture the moment with silly photos to immortalize your stylish creations.

Thrift Store Twist: For a hilarious twist, consider setting a low budget and hitting up a thrift store. Challenge yourselves to find the silliest outfits possible. Embrace the absurdity and enjoy a good laugh as you model your finds.

Spice It Up

Take it a step further by selecting intimate attire or costumes for each other to wear at home! This playful challenge can ignite some sparks and add excitement to your relationship.

Embrace the Experience

Remember, the key is to step outside your comfort zone. If you're usually a "tie guy," maybe today is the day to don some leather! If you're a "leggings gal," why not rock a dress or pantsuit instead?. Pick something that genuinely excites you to see your partner in. Encourage each other to be open-minded and embrace what the other has chosen. After all, confidence is the ultimate accessory, and it looks good on everyone!

Conversation Starters

To keep the laughter flowing and the conversation engaging, here are some fun questions to discuss while you're on your adventure:

- *If everything was flattering on you, what outrageous outfit would you dare to wear?*
- *If you could look like any celebrity for a day, who would it be and why?*
- *What's a style you've always wanted to try but never had the guts to?*
- *How does your outfit make you feel? What vibe are you going for?*

- *What's the funniest outfit you've ever worn, and what was the occasion?*

This activity not only helps you connect through laughter and shared experiences but also allows you both to discover new sides of each other's personalities and styles. Enjoy your stylish adventure together!

Book Club

What You'll Need

- A book that intrigues both of you or even a curated list of titles to explore together

Directions

Why not start a mini book club with just the two of you? Pick a book neither of you has read, nor take turns selecting a favorite to share. You don't have to read at the same time—read a chapter on your lunch break or listen to the audiobook version while commuting.

Then, take time to discuss it together over coffee or during a quiet evening. Books have a way of inspiring conversation, helping you learn about each other's perspectives, sense of humor, and what makes each other tick.

Ways to Make it Fun and Intimate

Try listening to a steamy audiobook, which can spark lighthearted or playful discussions. You can also pick a mystery or thriller and share your guesses on the outcome. Make it your tradition to read a chapter or two in bed, ending each night with a shared story.

Conversation Starters

- *What are some book characters you relate to and why?*
- *If you could meet any fictional character, who would it be?*
- *What book left a lasting impact on you?*

Spice It Up

Turn it into a cozy ritual—grab a blanket, some tea or wine, and dive into a story together. Or make it a themed evening based on the book's setting, like a small Italian dinner for a book set in Italy. Each book can open doors to a whole new way of enjoying each other's company, learning about each other's tastes, and creating lasting memories.

Amateur Detective

What You'll Need

- A mystery subscription service, like "Hunt a Killer," "Dear Holmes," or "Deadbolt Mystery Society."
- Optional: a notebook to jot down clues, and maybe a magnifying glass to get into character!

Directions

Dive into an immersive mystery together! Subscription boxes like these bring a thrilling storyline, clues, and suspects right to your living room. Pick one with a theme you both love and tackle it side by side. Imagine yourselves as detectives in a classic "whodunit" adventure, where every detail might hold the key to unlocking the mystery. True crime podcasts can also be a great add-on for a long car ride or a cozy evening indoors, helping you put your sleuthing skills to the test.

Spice it Up

Add a secret message for your partner using invisible ink (lemon juice and a Q-tip work perfectly). Write out something sweet or a hint about the case, then reveal it by gently heating the paper. This playful twist on leaving clues makes the experience even more mysterious!

Why It's Fun

If you were ever captivated by the mysteries solved by Nancy Drew, Sherlock Holmes, or Hercule Poirot, this is the night for you. It's an escape from the usual TV routine and a chance to connect over clues, theories, and "aha" moments. Plus, working together will give you that thrill of victory when you crack the case!

Conversation Starters

- *"Did you ever want to be a detective?"*
- *"What's the most mysterious thing that's happened to you?"*
- *"If you could ask one question to solve this case, what would it be?"*

Bonus Challenge

Dress the part! Throw on a trench coat, grab a notebook, and transform your space into a detective's office. It's a night of fun, laughs, and intrigue as you play detective and crack the case together.

Couples Tattoos

What You'll Need

- Body-safe pens (in a variety of colors or classic black)
- Tattoo ideas (browse websites for inspiration)

Directions

First, grab some body-safe pens designed specifically for temporary tattoos. Then, each of you can pick a design to draw on the other person. Try a meaningful symbol, a fun doodle, or even something totally goofy. Make it a surprise or collaborate on the design to make it a team effort.

For those less confident in their drawing skills, you can print out a stencil, cut it out, and trace it onto each other. Or, let this be a chance to just go wild and see what you come up with together! If you're thinking about a real tattoo in the future, this is a great opportunity to test a design.

Spice it up

Draw each other a "hidden" tattoo where only you two will know it's there. Explore designs that capture something unique about your relationship and imagine what kind of permanent tattoo you might consider getting together one day.

Conversation Starters

- *Would you ever get a tattoo? If you already have some, would you consider more?*
- *If you could get any design, what would it be? And why?*

- *How do you feel about piercings? Would you ever get one or find them appealing?*
- *Do you think tattoos or piercings can be sexy? Why or why not?*

Romantic Inspiration

Many beautiful love stories featuring less publicly famous individuals have captured attention due to their heartfelt and touching nature. These stories may not involve celebrities but reflect profound connections, resilience, and devotion. Here are a few examples of such love stories:

These love stories remind us that romance and commitment aren't reserved for the famous—they are found in people's quiet, everyday lives worldwide. Whether through small gestures, lifelong devotion, or standing by each other in the face of adversity, these couples show us the enduring beauty of love in all its forms.

Fred and Lorraine Desroches

- ***Their Story:*** *Fred Desroches, a retired police officer, touched hearts worldwide when he wrote a book of poems dedicated to his late wife, Lorraine, after she passed away. After 57 years of marriage, Lorraine's death left Fred heartbroken, and he began writing poems to cope with the grief. His book Lorraine, My Beautiful Angel is a tribute to their enduring love.*

- ***A Love of Devotion:*** *Their love story is one of lifelong devotion, where Fred describes his wife as his "one true love." Even after her passing, Fred's love for Lorraine shines through his words, reminding him how love can transcend even the most tremendous loss.*

Kayla and Cody Morin

- ***Their Story:*** *Kayla and Cody Morin, high school sweethearts from Colorado, made headlines when they planned an "epic" scavenger hunt proposal. Cody created an elaborate city-wide scavenger hunt for Kayla, leading her through meaningful* locations from their relationship, each stop including friends and family as clues. The destination was a surprise proposal in the park where they had their first date.

- **A Love of Creativity:** Cody's creative proposal became a viral sensation because it was personal and thoughtful, showing just how deeply he knew and loved Kayla. Their story is a reminder that love is often about the little details, and thoughtfulness, making life feel like an adventure no matter where you are.

Cathy and Marin

- **Their Story:** Cathy and Marin's love story began not in the bloom of youth but in the golden light of life's later chapters. At 58, Cathy had just made a fresh start in the vibrant city of New Orleans, leaving behind a lifetime of memories and stepping into a new era of discovery. Living in sunny Miami, Marin was also on her own journey, having raised two grown children and found peace with her past. Both had been married before, but it was in their 50s that they genuinely discovered their deepest selves—including their true sexuality, a revelation that felt freeing and empowering. When they met online, sparks flew instantly, and it was clear that they were two souls destined to cross paths at just the right time.

- **A Love of Late Blooming:** What started as messages filled with playful banter and deep conversations quickly blossomed into a romance that spanned miles. They danced between two cities for eight months, awaiting weekends filled with long walks under moonlit skies, impromptu jazz clubs, and shared laughter over wine and beignets in the French Quarter. Each visit deepened their connection, making it harder to say goodbye. They were like teenagers in love but with the wisdom and confidence of two people who had learned to embrace life fully. Finally, with hearts full of excitement, Marin moved to New Orleans, where she and

Cathy began their shared adventure. Together, they proved that romance isn't bound by age or circumstance—it's a joy that can be rediscovered at any stage, and sometimes, it's even sweeter the second time around.

Smell the Roses

What You'll Need

- Your local botanical garden or nearby park
- Picnic supplies (blanket, snacks, drinks)
- Art supplies (sketchbook, paints, or camera – whatever inspires you)
- Pen and paper

Directions

Spend a day in nature together – whether it's your local botanical garden, a scenic park, or a hidden gem that lets you connect in peace. Feel the fresh air, the warmth of the sun, and the scent of blooming flowers.

Make it a Date: Pack a cozy picnic lunch. Spread out the blanket, relax, and share a meal. Bring some light, fresh foods you both love.

Create Something Together: If you're feeling inspired, try capturing the beauty around you! Sketch a flower, paint the landscape, or even take turns photographing one another among the blooms. No art skills are required—just have fun and embrace each other's creativity!

Write a Love Note or Poem: After walking through the garden, jot down a few words or a short poem inspired by the day. Share it aloud, even if it's silly. The goal isn't perfection, just connection.

Unplug Completely: Leave your phones at home or in the car. It's all about immersing in each other's presence and the peace around you.

Remember, sometimes the best gift you can give is undivided attention, free from distractions.

Spice It Up

Bring a bit of that garden magic home! Scatter rose petals on the bed or the dining table to make any night feel special. It doesn't need to be a holiday – a thoughtful gesture goes a long way.

Why This Works

Spending intentional time outdoors not only boosts your health but also creates a tranquil space for you both to reconnect. Breathe, relax, and let nature bring out the best in each other.

Conversation Starters

Keep the laughs coming with these light-hearted questions:

- *Body Swap Fun:* "If we swapped bodies for a day, what's the first thing you would do?"
- *The Art of Disagreement:* "What's your favorite thing about the way we disagree?"
- *Our Pet's Take:* "If our pet (or plant) could talk, what would they say about our relationship? Or our eating habits?"

This gentle and playful activity reminds you both to slow down, laugh a little, and savor every moment together.

Murder Party

What You'll Need

- Friends & Guest List
- Dinner Menu/Plan
- A Theme with Optional Costumes
- **Character Assignments and a Murder Story:** *You can create a story yourself if you're feeling thrifty and creative. But for ease and a well-structured experience, consider purchasing a mystery package from Night of Mystery, which includes everything you need.*

Directions

Select a Theme & Plan Your Mystery: If crafting a mystery sounds daunting, a package from Night of Mystery offers a complete experience with character assignments, story details, and directions.

Send Invitations & Character Briefs: After you've finalized the guest list and story, send out the invitations and character briefs, letting each guest know who they'll be portraying.

Host the Dinner Party: Gather your guests for a dinner filled with suspense, clues, and delightful surprises. Embrace your roles, enjoy the evening, and let the mystery unravel.

Spice It Up

For added fun, stay in character even after your guests leave to keep the mystery alive a bit longer. It can be a unique way to end the night with an extra dose of intrigue!

Conversation Starters

- *Do you prefer hanging out with a few friends, or a large party? Why?*
- *Do you wish we had more friends?*
- *If you'd like to meet more couple friends, how do you think we could make that happen?*

Enjoy creating memorable moments and unraveling clues with your guests!

You're my Favorite

What You'll Need

- A list of everything your partner loves.
- A plan for a full day (or night) tailored to them.

Directions

Make a list of everything that makes your partner's heart beat a little faster—their favorite things to do, eat, watch, or listen to. Then, craft a day focused solely on their favorite things and show them just how well you know them. Think of it as a little love treasure hunt where each stop reflects something uniquely "them."

For the day

- **Start off strong:** Play their favorite playlist on the way to your first destination. It's not about your own preferences today—it's all about what makes them smile.
- **Dressed to impress:** Slip into their favorite outfit or style of yours that they love to see you in. You'll start the day off on the right foot, with a touch of extra thoughtfulness.
- **Go all in:** Plan stops at their favorite places, from a cozy café to that scenic overlook they love.

Then, at dinner

- Treat them to their favorite restaurant or make their favorite dish at home. It doesn't have to be extravagant—just heartfelt and thoughtful.

When the day wraps up, it's time to pass the baton. Switch roles! They get to show their appreciation by planning a day just for you.

Spice it Up

Why let it end with the day? Set the stage for a night all about them too. Light candles, queue up their favorite movie or show, or set the mood for an intimate, relaxing evening. The details don't need to be elaborating—they just need to say, "I see you, and I cherish you."

Conversation Starters

Let these prompts bring out some fresh insights and help you both feel connected:

- *"What's something you wish we got to do more often?"*
- *"If you could pick one thing to add to our lives to make it more fulfilling, what would it be?"*
- *"How can we create more space in our lives to focus on each other?"*

Remember: The day isn't about flashy spending; it's about showing your partner that you know and appreciate them better than anyone. These small, thoughtful gestures add up to a big reminder of how special they are to you.

Pub Crawl (or Bar Hop)

What You'll Need

- **Map or Route Planner:** Choose your stops around town or in a new place you're visiting. Mark the bars or pubs that serve unique cocktails, craft beers, or fun mocktails for a night of variety.

- **A Pair of Comfy Shoes is** essential for a night of walking, especially if you're hitting multiple spots. (Your feet will thank you later!)

- **A Designated Driver (or Ride Share App):** Prioritize safety so that you can fully enjoy the evening without worry.

- **Notebook or Phone Camera:** Capture your favorite drinks, new recipes, or memorable moments with your partner or group.

- **Appetite for Adventure:** Be ready to try new flavors and snack pairings, from savory tapas to exotic appetizers.

Directions

Plan Your Route: Take a few minutes to map out your ideal route. To maximize your time spent at each spot, consider locations that are walkable or a short drive apart. Include bars, pubs, and cafes known for their unique drink menus, and make sure there's something fun and different at each stop.

Get Sippin': At each location, try a new drink together—a cocktail you've never tasted, a mocktail with a twist, or a local beer you've been curious about. Share your thoughts on each one. Is it tangy, sweet, earthy, or surprising? Sip slowly and savor the moment with each other.

Snack Attack: Pair each drink with a small snack. Whether it's sliders, spicy wings, or a bowl of artisanal popcorn, let the snacks be part of the experience. Note which flavors work well together and which you'd try again.

Capture the Night: Snap photos of each drink and snack combo or write down any stand-out flavors or memorable moments. Did a bartender share a secret ingredient? Or did you both discover a new favorite? These little details will make for fun memories.

Add a Twist: Make it more exciting by creating a scoring system for each drink and snack. Rate them based on taste, presentation, and creativity. The winning drink might become the inspiration for a future at-home date night!

Spice It Up

Add a Personal Twist: Surprise your partner with a custom drink creation inspired by their favorite flavors. When you get to a stop, ask the bartender to make a custom cocktail or mocktail with your chosen ingredients and name it something personal!

Create a Drink Journal Together: After each stop, write down your thoughts on the drinks, flavors, and overall vibe of the place. This journal can become a keepsake, or you might use it to recreate your favorite drink at home for your next date night.

Why It Matters

Exploring new places and tasting new things together is more than just fun—it's a great way to create memories and bond over shared experiences. The thrill of discovering the perfect cocktail or snack you both love will bring you closer and add excitement to your relationship.

Conversation Starters

- What's the most unusual cocktail or mocktail you've tried?
- If you could invent a signature drink named after you, what would it taste like?
- What's your favorite memory from the night so far?

The Pub Crawl (or Bar Hop) experience is about enjoying the little things—flavors, laughs, and those moments of surprise that bring you closer. Just grab a drink and some good company, and let the night unfold!

Antiquing

What You'll Need

- **A Local Antique Market or Flea Market Map:** Find a nearby market that's known for its eclectic collection of treasures. The more stalls, the better!
- **Reusable Tote Bag or Backpack:** Handy for carrying your finds, from delicate trinkets to larger home decor.
- **Budget:** Set a budget beforehand or decide to buy only pieces that truly spark joy or have special meaning.
- **Curiosity and an Open Mind:** Some of the best finds are unexpected. Embrace the thrill of the hunt!
- **Coffee or a Favorite Beverage:** A bit of fuel for a day of treasure hunting—plus, it's nice to have something to sip while you browse.

Directions

Choose Your Market: Look for an antique or flea market that's known for its variety. Pick a weekend day to explore the aisles together. Some markets even have themes, so check if there's one that fits your interests!

Hunt for Hidden Gems: As you stroll, look for items that stand out to you both. Whether it's vintage jewelry, unique home decor, or a quirky item that sparks a laugh, enjoy sharing your discoveries. Talk about what catches your eye and why—it could reveal something new about each other's tastes!

Find a 'Couple's Treasure': Search for something meaningful that symbolizes your relationship. It could be an old love letter, a charming picture frame, or a vintage board game. Let your intuition guide you; finding something together makes it even more special.

Capture the Moment: Snap a few photos of each other exploring or taking a quick selfie with a fun discovery. These little moments will make for great memories.

Add a Twist: Choose a theme for the day, like "something blue," "vintage books," or "classic movie memorabilia." Make it a playful challenge to find items that fit the theme, adding an element of adventure to your antiquing date.

Spice It Up

Make It a Collection Day: If you share an interest, such as old postcards, vinyl records, or vintage kitchenware, focus on adding to your collection. Look for items with a story and take turns choosing which pieces to bring home.

Create a 'Mystery Gift' Tradition: During the trip, secretly pick out something special for each other. When you get home, reveal your gifts—it's a fun way to add an element of surprise and thoughtfulness to the experience.

Why It Matters

Antiquing isn't just about the items you find; it's about the time you spend together, exploring and learning about each other's tastes. Sharing in the excitement of the hunt and finding little treasures builds connection and makes for a memorable date.

Conversation Starters

- What's the most interesting thing you've found today?
- If you could pick any decade to live in based on its style, what would it be?

- What's a dream item you hope to find one day at an antique market?

Antiquing is all about discovery—both of treasures and each other. So grab a bag, hit the market, and see what hidden gems await!

Museum Visit

What You'll Need

- **Museum Tickets or Membership Passes:** Choose a museum that interests you, whether it's art, history, science, or something unique to your area.
- **Notebook or Phone Notes App:** Jot down facts about the exhibits and any questions or ideas that come to mind.
- **Curiosity and a Sense of Wonder:** Every exhibit has a story waiting to be discovered—embrace it!
- **Comfy Shoes and Museum-Appropriate Attire:** For a day of strolling and exploring, dress comfortably and bring a sense of adventure.

Directions

Select Your Museum: Pick a museum you're both excited to explore. It could be an art gallery, a natural history museum, or even a quirky local museum with offbeat collections.

Do Your Research: Before your visit, look up 10 interesting facts about the museum's exhibits. Choose ones that intrigue you, have a funny backstory, or connect to something personal. The goal is to share and surprise each other with fun tidbits along the way.

Explore Together: Once inside, seek out the objects or displays from your list. As you find each one, take turns sharing your 10 fascinating facts. You'll both get to see the exhibit in a new light and can bond over your shared reactions.

Engage with the Artifacts: Ask questions, comment on each other's facts, and take photos together. This is a great chance to learn more about each other's interests and see how each of you interprets the world around you.

Add a Twist: Make it a friendly challenge! At the end of your museum visit, vote on the best or most surprising fact shared. The winner could receive a small treat, such as a coffee or a souvenir from the gift shop.

Spice It Up

Choose a Themed Museum Date: Choose a unique or unusual museum, such as a museum of oddities, a space observatory, or an outdoor sculpture garden. Trying something out of the ordinary makes for a more adventurous experience.

Create a Mini Museum Tour for Each Other: In advance, secretly pick a few exhibits to "guide" your partner through. Add personal touches to your facts—why does this piece stand out to you, or does it remind you of something from your relationship? It's a thoughtful way to share memories and emotions through the exhibits.

Why It Matters

Exploring a museum together goes beyond seeing artifacts; it's about learning, sharing, and connecting on a deeper level. Discovering new facts side-by-side fosters a sense of closeness and can spark conversations that last a lifetime.

Conversation Starters

- What's something you saw today that surprised you?
- If you could take home any exhibit, what would it be and why?
- What kind of museum would you love to create together?

A museum visit is a journey of discovery—not just of art and history, but of each other. So grab a notebook, wander the halls, and let your shared curiosity lead the way!

Made in United States
Troutdale, OR
03/15/2025

29783379R00090